SQUADRONS!

No. 50

THE HAWKER
TEMPEST MK V
- THE NEW ZEALANDERS -

PHIL H. LISTEMANN

ISBN: 979-1096490-84-4

Copyright

© 2021 Philedition - Phil Listemann

revised July 2024

Colour profiles: Gaetan Marie/Bravo Bravo Aviation

GLOSSARY OF TERMS

PERSONEL :
(AUS)/RAF: Australian serving in the RAF
(BEL)/RAF: Belgian serving in the RAF
(CAN)/RAF: Canadian serving in the RAF
(CZ)/RAF: Czechoslovak serving in the RAF
(NFL)/RAF: Newfoundlander serving in the RAF
(NL)/RAF: Dutch serving in the RAF
(NZ)/RAF: New Zealander serving in the RAF
(POL)/RAF: Pole serving in the RAF
(RHO)/RAF: Rhodesian serving in the RAF
(SA)/RAF: South African serving in the RAF
(US)/RAF - RCAF : American serving in the RAF or RCAF

RANKS
G/C : Group Captain
W/C : Wing Commander
S/L : Squadron Leader
F/L : Flight Lieutenant
F/O : Flying Officer
P/O : Pilot Officer
W/O : Warrant Officer
F/Sgt : Flight Sergeant
Sgt : Sergeant
Cpl : Corporal
LAC : Leading Aircraftman

OTHER
ATA: Air Transport Auxiliary
CO : Commander
DFC : Distinguished Flying Cross
DFM : Distinguished Flying Medal
DSO : Distinguished Service Order
Eva. : Evaded
ORB : Operational Record Book
OTU : Operational Training Unit
PoW : Prisoner of War
PAF: Polish Air Force
RAF : Royal Air Force
RAAF : Royal Australian Air Force
RCAF : Royal Canadian Air Force
RNZAF : Royal New Zealand Air Force
SAAF : South African Air Force
s/d: Shot down
Sqn : Squadron
† : Killed

CODENAMES - OFFENSIVE OPERATIONS - FIGHTER COMMAND

CIRCUS:
Bombers heavily escorted by fighters, the purpose being to bring enemy fighters into combat.

RAMROD:
Bombers escorted by fighters, the primary aim being to destroy a target.

RANGER:
Large formation freelance intrusion over enemy territory with aim of wearing down enemy figthers.

RHUBARD:
Freelance fighter sortie against targets of opportunity.

ROADSTEAD:
Dive bombing and low level attacks on enemy ships at sea or in harbour

RODEO:
A fighter sweep without bombers.

SWEEP:
An offensive flight by fighters designed to draw up and clear the enemy from the sky.

THE HAWKER TEMPEST MK V

The Hawker Tempest was derived from the Typhoon. Hawker Aircraft reached the conclusion its heavyweight fighter, the Typhoon, while still in development, suffered from a major limitation to its performance and further work on the wing section could help improve overall performance.

Due to changing priorities during the Battle of Britain, the design of the new wing was not commenced until September 1941, but it provoked some deep changes in the overall design. This new thin wing meant alternative space for fuel had to be found; this was achieved by moving the engine forward and inserting a tank between the firewall and the oil tank. That also led to the design of a new undercarriage unit and Hawker took this opportunity to equip the new fighter with the latest version of the Napier Sabre engine, the Mk.IV. A contract was placed in November 1941 for two prototypes named, at the time, Typhoon Mk.II.

In the following spring, problems with the Sabre forced Hawker to find alternatives. As various engines were under development, four more prototypes were soon ordered. One would be fitted with the Sabre IV as initially planned, one with the Sabre II (as was installed in the Typhoon), two with the Rolls-Royce Griffon 61, and two with the Bristol Centaurus when it became available. Following this decision, the Typhoon Mk.II was renamed in August and mark numbers were allocated to the different variants: Mk.I with the Sabre IV, Mk.II with the Centaurus IV, Mk.III with the Griffon IIB, Mk.IV with the Griffon 61, and Mk.V with the Sabre II. The Tempest was born. Owing to various delays with the Sabre IV and Centaurus engines, and the redesign necessary for the Griffon installation, the prototype of the Mk.V, HM595, was ready for its maiden flight well before the others. This took place on 2 September 1942. It was beyond satisfactory from the start, and production was soon launched, while the Marks III and IV were soon abandoned when the Griffon was ear-marked for the Spitfire; the Tempest Mk.I followed suit as the Mk.V entered service and immediately proved its worth. Only the Mk.II would make it into RAF service, but after the war ended.

The first production Tempest V flew on 21 June 1943 as part of an initial order of 100 airframes (**JN729–JN877**). These aircraft were known as the 'Mark V Series 1' and were distinguished from the later 'Mark V Series 2' by having the longer-barrel Hispano Mk.II cannon that protruded beyond the wings' leading edges. The first series was delivered to operational units from January 1944 as pure fighters, not fighter-bombers, as the modifications required to carry bombs and fire rocket projectiles (RPs) were not expected until the 150th example off the line. This first batch was followed by a second lot of 300 aircraft drawn from a Typhoon order (**EJ504–EJ896**), and a batch of 130 airframes (**NV639–NV793**) that was later amended to 410 (**NV917–NX482**). However, only 69 of the latter batch were delivered as Tempest Mk.Vs; the remainder were built as Mk.VIs after the war (the Mk.VI was a tropicalised version of the Mk.V). A final batch of 250 (**SN102–SN416**) began to be delivered a few weeks before VE-Day, but the last 49 were cancelled in September 1945.

The Mk.V prototype, HM595, seen here at Langley, the Hawker Aircraft's factory and test airfield, west of London. The Tempest Mk.V was ready to fly long before the Mk.I and Mk.II prototypes. The evolution from the Typhoon is clearly visible in the original Typhoon tail unit and the early 'car-door' style canopy. *(CT Collection)*

HM595 under test at the A&AEE, still with the original Typhoon-style canopy but with a larger tailplane plus interim fin extention for handling trials. The white line along the rear fuselage was a datum line for photographic reference during tests. *(CT Collection)*

4

The first production Tempest V, JN729, around the time of its first flight on 21 June 1943. *(CT Collection)*

In all, 801 Tempests were built. This was enough to equip eight operational squadrons during the war: Nos 3, 33, 56, 80, 222, 274, 486 (NZ), and 501 Squadrons, and, partially, the Fighter Interception Unit, and the type was heavily involved in the anti-V-1 campaign (of which close to 800 were destroyed by Tempests). Moving to the Continent and incorporated into the Second Tactical Air Force (2TAF), the Tempest proved its value and by VE-Day about 350 enemy aircraft had been claimed as destroyed or probably destroyed. About 23,000 operational sorties were carried out in about a year of combat. However, 250 Tempests were struck off charge for one reason or another during the same laps of time. After the war, the type remained in service with the RAF until the end of the forties. The first squadron to convert to the new type was No. 486 (NZ) Squadron and was the only non-British unit to fly it.

Tempest EJ743 of Series 2, identified as such by the short barrel 20mm cannons.

Above, a Typhoon and Tempest of 486 Sqn side by side in early 1944, making the comparison between the two types much easier. Left, a photo of the undersurfaces showing the special identification markings applied to avoid confusion with Fw190s. The same markings were applied to the Typhoon early on.
(CT Collection)

Victories - confirmed or probable claims: 62.0 + 242.33 V-1s

Number of sorties: *ca.* **5,350**

First operational sortie:
01.05.44

Total aircraft written-off: 48

Last operational sortie:
05.05.45

Aircraft lost on operations: 45
Aircraft lost in accidents: 3

Squadron code letters:
SA

COMMANDING OFFICERS

S/L James H. Iremonger	RAF No. 33342	RAF	...	11.12.44
S/L Arthur E. Umbers (†)	NZ404003	RNZAF	11.12.44	14.02.45
S/L Keith G. Taylor-Cannon (†)	NZ412284	RNZAF	15.02.45	13.04.45
S/L Warren E. Schrader	NZ411944	RNZAF	21.04.45	02.05.45
S/L Cornelius J. Sheddan	NZ412358	RNZAF	02.05.45	...

SQUADRON USAGE

The squadron was New Zealand's second fighter unit in the UK. It formed in March 1942 as a night fighter squadron operating with the Turbinlite Havocs of No. 1453 Flight (see *SQUADRONS! 24*), but the concept proved unsuccessful. It soon changed to the day fighter role and converted to the Typhoon in July 1942. The squadron operated the Typhoon until January 1944 when conversion to the Tempest was considered. At the time, 486 was based at Tangmere and under the command of S/L James H. Iremonger since a few days, a British officer. On 14 January, three Tempests were received for familiarisation purposes (JN733/X, JN735/Y and JN738/Z). They were followed by two more on the 21st, JN739/W and JN743/V, while operational duties continued with the Typhoons. The aim was to create a Tempest Wing with Nos 3 and 56 Squadrons. That seems to have been premature as, at the end of February, 486 made another move, this time to Drem (the squadron had moved to Beaulieu to operate in the Middle Wallop sector at the end of January), leaving its Tempests to 3 Squadron, owing to a lack of aircraft, and continued to fly the Typhoon.

This arrangement did not last long, however, as, in April, the squadron converted for good; the first Tempest of the new batch arrived early in the month following an Armament Practice Camp at Ayr, the squadron being temporarily based at Castle Camps. Conversion consumed the month and, on the 29th, 486 moved to Newchurch, midway between Hastings and Dover, with its sixteen Tempests where it joined 3 Squadron (now fully equipped with the new aircraft). The third squadron of 150 Airfield (renamed 150 Wing in May), 56, was still flying the Typhoon; its conversion occurred in June. Two days before the move, 486 lost its first Tempest when, after an engine failure during a practice flight, F/O H.M. Mason was obliged to make a forced landing at Castle Camps, wrecking the aircraft in the process; he escaped unscathed. Now based at Newchurch, the first Tempest sorties were carried out on 1 May. Flying Officers J.G. Wilson and W.A. Hart went on patrol off Dungeness, but the flight ended badly for Wilson. His engine over-speeded and he had to make the unit's second forced landing in four days, crashing near Staple where the Tempest broke into several pieces. The aircraft was too damaged to repair, but Wilson was unhurt. Other patrols were flown the next day and, on the 3rd, the first offensive sweep was carried out. Eight Tempests led by the CO took off at 14.05, joining nine aircraft of 3 Squadron for *Ramrod 826*. It was a fighter sweep over the north-east of France in connection with a series of bombing raids by medium bombers. The engines continued to give trouble as the CO was obliged to return early, leaving F/L H.N. Sweetman to lead for the rest of the uneventful op. Over the next few days, 486 flew various patrols or shipping recces, and, more rarely, some Rangers or Ramrods (each involving several aircraft). More important assignments were also completed with a Roadstead on the 18th, two fighter sweeps in the Lille area on the 19th and 20th, and another sweep over Cambrai on the 24th. Two more ops were flown on the 29th near the Berck–Saint-Pol and Furnes–Lille areas but, excluding some targets of opportunity, May was simply uneventful despite 180 operational sorties being flown.

James Henry Iremonger

RAF No. 33342

Already serving with the RAF when war broke out, Johnny Iremonger had spent the early years of his career in the Far East, initially flying Hawker Audaxes as an army co-operation pilot with No 20 Squadron. With the outbreak of war with Japan, he switched to the fighter role and was posted, in January 1942, to No 5 Squadron, still flying Audaxes, as the unit was about to convert to the Curtiss Mohawk. A few weeks later, he was posted to command No 17 Squadron. He led 17 until December 1942 when he was posted to No 224 Group HQ as a wing commander. He returned to the UK in the summer of 1943 and started a new tour, reverting to squadron leader, initially posted as supernumerary to No 197 Squadron, a Typhoon unit, in October 1943 before joining No 486 (NZ) Squadron in January 1944 to supervise the unit's transition to the Tempest. He led the squadron during the V-1 campaign, claiming two destroyed (one shared) himself during the summer. Iremonger eventually left 486 in December 1944 for an HQ position and was awarded the DFC in January 1945. He remained in the RAF after the war.

Hawker Tempest Mk. V JN763
No. 486 (NZ) Squadron
Squadron Leader JH Iremonger
Newchurch (UK), June 1944

Tempest JN738/SA-Z, one of the first issued to 486 Sqn in January 1944. It was transferred to 3 Sqn in February.

The first days of June continued the trend with only a handful of patrols or shipping recces carried out. On D-Day, the squadron was kept in reserve at full readiness all day and was ultimately not required, except for routine shipping/weather recces and shipping patrols, until dusk when elements of the wing patrolled the Bay of Seine and landed at Ford. The next day, several scrambles were carried out, but all interceptions proved friendly. On the 8th, however, 486 and 3 Squadrons went on the offensive for the first time since D-Day with a sweep performed in the Caen area just after midday. Some Bf109s were sighted and attacked by W/C R.P. Beamont and 3 Squadron while 486 remained as top cover. Later in the afternoon, another sweep was ordered near the Fécamp–Amiens area but was cancelled before the aircraft reached the French coast owing to adverse weather. Two days later, the 10th, was also a busy day with sweeps and patrols carried out but luck was not on the squadron's side as, on the first sweep (targeting Le Havre), a Tempest was attacked by a Spitfire; fortunately, the attacker broke off before it was too late. On the second sweep of the day, which took place late in the evening, the Tempest flown by P/O F.B. Lawless, while heading for Caen, developed engine trouble to the point he had to ditch in the Channel. Fortunately, he was only slightly injured and was soon picked up by an ASR launch. That was the first ditching made by a Tempest. The rest of the formation continued on and F/L W.L. Miller was later caught by flak; his aircraft was damaged badly enough to necessitate a safe forced landing at Ford. The Tempest was soon repaired. During the next few days, 486 flew ops every day but all proved uneventful. A major event soon changed the unit's fate. The German V-1 had been introduced into combat and the first of them passed over before midnight on the 13th. This new threat had to be stopped and Air Defence Great Britain (formerly Fighter Command) switched to anti-Diver patrols, calling on the Tempest Wing to intercept the flying bombs. The first such patrols for 486 were carried out on the 16th; 44 were flown that day and the first V-1s spotted and destroyed. The very first one was credited to F/Sgt B.J. O'Connor who shot it down around midday between Rye and Dungeness. Forty minutes later, P/O K. McCarthy shot one down north of Rye, the V-1 exploding on the ground. The Tempest soon proved a remarkable tool in the V-1 hunt, especially in Kiwi hands, 486 scoring every day until the end of the month. Two were destroyed on the 17th, twelve on the 18th. The best day would be the 23rd with sixteen claims filed. For June alone, close to 100 V-1s were destroyed by the Kiwis. With such a scoreboard, some pilots soon became V-1 aces, like F/O Ray Cammock with 8.5, F/O Owen 'Ginger' Eagleson with eight, P/O 'Dan' Danzey with seven, Pilot Officers McCarthy and 'Black Mac' McCaw with six each, and F/O 'Bev' Hall and F/Sgt 'Sid' Short with five each. The Kiwis flew close to 800 sorties that month, but, despite appearances, it was far from a walk in the park. The squadron did not make it through the month unscathed. On the 22nd, F/O T.M. Fenton ran out of fuel on patrol and crashed at Newchurch; the aircraft was only good for scrap. The 28th was a really bad day. Late at night, F/O S.S. Williams and F/Sgt W.T. Wright were on patrol when they spotted and attacked a V-1; the attack was not decisive. Wright, however, was hit by friendly anti-aircraft fire. He was last heard to say he had been fired on and that he had been hit and was going to attempt a forced landing. He finally crashed into the sea off Beachy Head. Williams's aircraft was also hit but returned to base. Earlier that day, Lawless crashed in the vicinity of Rye after flying through a V-1 that exploded after he opened fire. Two days later, it was the turn of 'Sid' Short to see his Tempest damaged by debris from a V-1 he had just shot down; he crashed at the end of the runway, sealing the fate of his aircraft.

In July, the V-1 campaign continued and 486 beat another record by achieving close to 900 sorties. That month, 115 V-1s were destroyed by the Kiwis and new names appeared on the aces list (Flying Officers J.R. Cullen, W.A. Hart, G.J.M. Hooper, and W.A. Kalka, Pilot Officers F.B. Lawless, W.L. Miller and B.J. O'Connor, W/O C.J. 'Jimmy' Sheddan, and F/O S.S. Williams) while the June aces continued to increase their tallies. This impressive record had a high cost. On 1 July, P/O K. McCarthy crashed in a wood near Hastings after an engine failure during an anti-Diver patrol. He was seriously injured. On 3 July, Miller baled out of his Tempest after the engine failed during a night patrol, the visibility being too poor to consider a forced landing. The next day, Williams crashed when his undercarriage refused to deploy upon returning from a night patrol. He was unhurt but the Tempest could not be repaired. The next day, Sheddan, after destroying two V-1s, started to attack a third when a spent shell hit his air intake. The Tempest was wrecked in the forced landing at Netherfield and Sheddan seriously injured. After several days without major incident, 486 began another bad run of luck. On the 20th, W/O S.J. Short was fired on by Allied flak during a patrol and his engine hit. He crashed at Deanland, emerging unhurt from a machine too damaged to repair. Then, in two days, the squadron lost three Tempests. The first, on the 23rd, was lost when P/O W.A.L. Trott returned to base with engine trouble after destroying two V-1s. He made a forced landing at Stonecross. The Tempest did not survive the crash, but Trott was unhurt. Then, the next day, Kalka and F/L N.J. Powell suffered the same misadventure when engine failures led to forced landings (six miles north of Friston for Kalka and near Snargate for Powell). Both pilots were safe, but their Tempests were wrecked. Flight Lieutenant E.W. Tanner's aircraft suffered the same fate when its brakes seized on landing at Newchurch. Worse was to come as, on the last day of the month during a patrol, F/Sgt A.A .Wilson collided near Brexhill with a Spitfire XIV from 91 Squadron. Both pilots were killed. Forty-five more V-1s were claimed in August, the last on 31 August by O'Connor. At the end of the hunt, the top scorers were Eagleson with 21, followed by Cammock with 20.5; four more pilots scored ten V-1s or more. Three Tempests were written off in August however. The first was flown by Ray Cammock on the 10th; just after take-off, he experienced an engine failure and subsequently made a forced landing at south west of Battle. He was safe, but the same could not be said for F/Sgt J.W. Waddell who crashed during an anti-Diver patrol on the 17th. The Tempest crashed into high ground near Tenterden, killing Waddell instantly. The real circumstances of the crash were never established but it seems that the poor visibility was responsible. While the last V-1 was destroyed on 31 August, 486 continued to fly anti-Diver patrols until 4 September. It then switched back to the more aggressive task of fighter sweeps, escorts and seeking out V-2 sites. September was uneventful until the 19th when the wing moved to Matlask in anticipation of another move, this time to the Continent; for this reason the wing was placed under 2TAF command on the 28th. This move was part of the reorganisation of 2TAF, the Tempest Wing replacing the Mustangs of No. 122 Wing, which was recalled to the UK. The squadron was based at B.60/Grimbergen in Belgium with 3 and 56; the Tempest squadrons became the new flying units of 122 Wing. Wing Commander Beamont made the move too and remained wing leader. The CO was G/C P.G. Jameson, a New Zealand ace, who had had an eventful war having survived the Norwegian campaign, the sinking of HMS *Glorious*, the Battle of Britain, and Dieppe. Patrols and armed recces began immediately, especially in the Arnhem area where the British had recently launched an airborne operation. It would not be long before the Luftwaffe was encountered and the first kills recorded. On 30 September, F/L

S/L Iremonger standing on Tempest JN763/SA-F in June 1944. *(CT Collection)*

Tempests JN754/SA-A and JN801/SA-L in full D-Day markings at Newchurch during the early stages of the V-1 campaign. Below, the left side of S/L Iremonger's JN763/SA-F in June 1944. The squadron leader pennant was only worn on the left side. *(CT Collection)*

Sequential camera gun images showing the destruction of a V-1 by F/L J. McCaw on 15 July 1944. *(McCaw family via P. Sortehaug)*

Williams was leading a patrol in the Arnhem area at 5000 feet when he spotted a single Bf109 flying east at 200/300 feet. He immediately reported to the top cover leader that he was going down to attack with his section. Williams broke formation and the Bf109 turned towards him, climbing slightly. Williams tried to get behind it but lost height in the process. He made various steep turns, still at about 200 feet above the Bf109, but it kept turning in to him until he was in a good position for a two-second burst with 95° deflection from about 600 yards. No strikes were seen and the Bf109 briefly disappeared from view. The German re-appeared from under the Tempest's nose, no longer turning, but climbing slightly and emitting glycol from its starboard radiator; the engine burst into flames. The Bf109 lost height and the pilot baled out at about 400/500 feet just before his aircraft crashed into a wood and blew up. This was the squadron's first confirmed kill of a manned aircraft since its conversion to the Tempest.

On 1 October, the squadron moved with the wing to B.80/Volkel in the Netherlands from where it continued armed recces and patrols, which proved to be full of danger. The first half of the month was difficult. On the 1st, two aircraft experienced engine trouble. While F/L K.G. Taylor-Cannon managed to get back home, P/O B.M. Hall had to make a forced landing just short of base, fortunately without major consequences for him or his aircraft. A few days later, on the 6th, during the course of an armed recce north-east of Arnhem, a goods train and about twenty trucks were attacked. Flight Lieutenant Cammock was hit by flak fired from the surrounding area. While at 500 feet, his engine caught fire and the Tempest ploughed directly into the rear of the train; Cammock was probably killed in the crash. The next day, F/O W.A. Hart was also hit while attacking a goods train south-east of Wesel. Luck was with him, however, as his engine only seized and, as he was flying at 2000 feet, he was high enough to bale out successfully, albeit straight into German hands. Returning from the same attack, W/O W.A. Bailey's engine started giving him trouble and he made a forced landing at Langstraat, in the vicinity of Volkel. He was soon back at base but the Tempest was eventually struck off charge owing to the considerable damage it sustained. Another Tempest was hit by flak three days later, but F/L E.W. Tanner managed to save himself and the aircraft with a nice forced landing near the Nijmegen bridge. The next day, the wing suffered a body blow when the wing leader, W/C R.P. Beamont was shot down and made a PoW. He was replaced by W/C J.B. Wray. Things calmed down after that, even though further engine troubles were reported, and the situation remained stable until the end of the month with about 350 sorties carried out. Aerial encounters were rare even though some sightings were made, including of the latest German threat, the Me262, a jet aircraft. On the 28th, luck was on 486's side. Late in the afternoon, some Me262s were observed approaching base from the south. Two were attacked with no obvious results by F/O R.J. Danzey who was returning home alone with a duff engine; he came across another five and managed to hit one from extreme range. He was then forced to break off when threatened from the rear. The Me262 was credited as damaged.

The rhythm of operations was maintained in November. No loss was recorded, but the squadron's scoreboard increased. On the

486 Squadron posing at the height of the V-1 campaign in July 1944:
On the fuselage, left to right: W/O O.D. Eagleson, W/O A.H. Bailey (†26.03.45), F/O H.M. Mason, Pilot Officers W.A.L. Trott and F.B. Lawless, F/L J.H. McCaw, W/O J.H. Stafford, F/L L.J. Appleton and F/Sgt H.N. Steedman.
On the wing, left to right: F/Sgt J.W. Waddell (†17.08.44), and Flying Officers S.S. Williams (†22.12.44) and F/O R.J. Cammock (†06.10.44).
On the box: Pilot Officers J.G. Wilson and R.D. Bremner.
Standing, left to right: Flying Officers W.H. Cole (Adj, British) and W.J.H. Sayers (MO, British), Flight Lieutenants J.R. Cullen (PoW 04.05.45) and V.StC. Cooke, P/O B.M. Hall (†27.12.44), S/L J.H. Iremonger (CO), Flying Officers W.A. Hart (PoW 07.10.44) and R.J. Danzey, and Flight Lieutenants E.W. Tanner and H.N. Sweetman.
Kneeling: F/O W.L. Miller and W/O W.A. Kalka (†25.03.45). *(JR Cullen via P. Sortehaug)*

Arthur Ernest UMBERS
NZ404003

'Spike' Umbers joined the RNZAF in November 1940. Trained in Canada, he sailed for the UK during the summer of 1941 and completed his course at No 53 OTU. He was posted to No 74 (Trinidad) Squadron in April 1941. In March 1942, when the second RNZAF fighter unit in Britain, No 486 (NZ) Squadron, was formed, he was posted in. He did not open his score until December that year when he shared in a Do217 while flying a Typhoon. In September 1943, now a flight commander, he was sent for a rest, having completed his tour, and was awarded the DFC. He returned to operations in April 1944 as a flight commander, flying Tempests, with No 3 Squadron where he destroyed about nineteen V-1s (three of which were shared) and received a Bar to his DFC (in July). In December 1944, he was again posted to 486, but this time as OC. He claimed three confirmed victories in January 1945 alone to bring his total to five confirmed (one shared), two probables (one shared), three aircraft damaged (one shared) and about twenty V-1s destroyed. Sadly, on 14 February 1945, while conducting an armed reconnaissance over Germany, he was shot down by flak and killed.

Hawker Tempest Mk. V EJ627
No. 486 (NZ) Squadron
B.80/Volkel (Netherlands), December 1944

19th, while on standing patrol, the formation was in the Rheine area when two Me262s were seen preparing for take-off from Rheine aerodrome. Led by F/L Taylor-Cannon, the Tempests dived and strafed the two jets, Taylor-Cannon and Eagleson probably destroying one while the second was claimed as damaged on the ground by P/O J. Steedman. Flight Lieutenant Taylor-Cannon would again be in the spotlight a few days later. On an early morning patrol, two Ju188s were encountered over an airfield to the east of Münster. One was just in the landing pattern, but the other appeared to be having some difficulty getting its undercarriage down. Flight Lieutenants Taylor-Cannon and Williams both fired on the latter and appeared to have hit the pilot for the aircraft pulled up vertically, blazing end to end; it was then seen to explode and a single parachute open. Steedman attacked the other Ju188, seeing strikes in the cockpit area, whereupon the aircraft collided with a tree, which was knocked over. The bomber then skidded along the ground, leaving a long furrow. The first Ju188 was credited as destroyed, and shared by the two pilots, but the second one, although initially claimed as destroyed, ultimately, and somewhat bizarrely, was only credited as a probable. Because of non-favourable weather, the number of sorties dropped to 250 in December, a month which also saw a change of command; S/L Iremonger was posted out on the 11th, tour expired. He was replaced by F/L A.E. Umbers from 3 Squadron. The first three weeks of the month were uneventful until F/L S. Williams was shot down and killed by flak near Vreden during a Ranger on the 22nd. He was avenged on Christmas Day. While flying a patrol in the Julich–Malmedy area, the squadron, led by the CO, was flying south of Aachen at 10,000 feet when, an hour into the flight, F/O J.H. Stafford and P/O P.D. Bremner spotted a Me262 at 11,000 feet flying west at 1500 yards range. The squadron climbed, but Stafford lost it in the sun; the Me262 soon came out of sun travelling north at high speed; Stafford broke up towards him and commenced firing at extreme range, continuing into 400 yards. He saw pieces fall away from the left nacelle. As the Me262 passed over, several red balls fell from it and the aircraft slowed considerably. Stafford got in behind as it started a moderate turn to the left. He closed the Me262 to 600 yards and fired again. The jet straightened out of the turn as he fired and dived, leaving a trail of white smoke. The Me262 rapidly built up speed and Stafford chased, firing occasional bursts. The jet pulled up and did a slow roll, straightening out as Stafford fired again. The Me262 then rolled on its back and Stafford saw the pilot bale out; the parachute did not open properly. The Me262 crashed and exploded seven miles from Aachen. Stafford was accompanied throughout the engagement by Bremner who also managed to fire at the Me262. For this reason, the Me262 was shared between the two Kiwis. The next day saw a collision between two aircraft, one flown by F/O C.J. MacDonald and the other by P/O B.J. O'Connor. That happened during another patrol of the same area as the day before. Once more, an Me262 was sighted and, in the hurry to get at it, the two Tempests clipped one another. Luck was with the Kiwis as no one was hurt; MacDonald parachuted to safety and O'Connor made a forced landing in the American lines. The following day, a major encounter for 2TAF took place. It all began with several armed recces over the Paderborn area around midday. Another Tempest squadron had already shot down four Fw190s when 486 arrived on the scene. The Kiwis were made aware by the controller that enemy air-

Tempest NV753/SA-J was issued to 486 Sqn in February 1945. It was mainly flown by P/O W.J. Shaw during the final weeks of the war. Shaw made his last claims flying this aircraft.

Volkel, during the winter of 1944–45, showing Tempests of 486 Sqn taxiing out for their next sortie over Germany.
Above, NV937/SA-C stayed with 486 for just two weeks. After striking trees near Paderborn, the Tempest left the squadron for repairs and never returned.
(KA Smith via P. Sortehaug)

craft were in the vicinity. Indeed, the squadron was soon under attack by about forty Fw190 and Bf109s. A furious dogfight ensued, a real challenge because it was soon discovered the Fw190s were the latest long-nose versions, but the Kiwis eventually got the advantage. Flight Lieutenants Tanner and Taylor-Cannon each claimed one Fw190 shot down as did F/O K.A. Smith and P/O S.J. Short. Two more claims were also credited to Tanner and F/O B.M. Hall for a Bf109 probably destroyed and another damaged respectively. The latter made his claim just before being shot down and killed by Fw190s.

The Luftwaffe attacked various Allied airfields on 1 January 1945. An armed recce led by the CO was already in the air when they were recalled at Arnhem to mix it up with the Luftwaffe over the Eindhoven area. They dropped their extra fuel tanks and the formation of eight Tempests rushed toward the town. Three Fw190s were sighted, two at 6000 feet and the one very low flying north towards Helmond. The Tempests split up and S/L Umbers chose the 190 on the deck. He opened fire from 300 yards and saw immediate strikes on the wing roots and fuselage. Black and white smoke streamed back from the Fw190 as it dramatically slowed down, forcing Umbers to pull up violently to avoid a collision. The fate of the Fw190 was sealed and Umbers was able to watch it crash and burst into flames. Immediately after, he saw a solitary Bf109 about a mile away flying east at 1500 feet. The German pilot spotted the two Tempests, immediately dived to ground level and attempted to join a gaggle of twenty other Bf109s in the vicinity. Umbers opened fire just as the pilot turned but saw no hits. The Bf109 straightened out with the main formation which then broke violently. Umbers was able to follow and, when the German straightened out, fired a short burst from 100 yards, obtaining hits on the cockpit, right wing root and fuselage. The Bf109's right wheel dropped, its speed fell off and, as it began to disappear under the Tempest's nose, Umbers saw the aircraft hit the ground and explode. The CO was not the only one to score that morning; P/O C.J. Sheddan claimed one Fw190 destroyed, F/O W.A.L. Trott and P/O G.J.M. Hooper claimed an Fw190 destroyed and Bf109 damaged each, while P/O J. Steedman claimed an Fw190 as damaged. The Kiwis suffered no loss. While the Luftwaffe had attempted to neutralise 2TAF and the US Ninth Air Force for a while, the operation failed, Allied losses being quickly replaced, something the Germans could not do as easily. The routine of ops returned in the hours following the attack. The squadron flew various armed recces over the next few days, the weather preventing much flying, but the Kiwis scored against targets of opportunity. On the 13th, 486 was flying an armed recce in the Saint Vith area when they were fired on by mistake by American anti-aircraft batteries near Euskirchen. The flak was accurate and three Tempests were hit badly enough to abruptly end their flight. The CO crashed near Verviers in the American lines, while P/O W. Kalka had to evacuate his aircraft. Flight Lieutenant L.J. Appleton made a forced landing near Euskirchen, seriously wounded in the neck and face. He was initially posted missing and it would take a fortnight to determine his fate when he was transferred to the 8th British General Hospital in Brussels. His war was over and, upon recovery, he was sent home. Two other Tempests were also hit but the pilots succeeded in returning to base. Despite this bad experience, the squadron was up again the next day for another armed recce, this time over the Paderborn area. Around midday, a Bf109 and Fw190 were sighted flying low, three miles north of Münster. The Tempests went after them immediately. The Bf109 was attacked by F/O C.J. McDonald and shot down. A couple of minutes later, two more Bf109s and an Fw190 were sighted flying north-west at ground level, three miles west of Münster this time. They were engaged and the fate of one Fw190 was sealed by W/O J.E. Wood. These two claims helped to calm the anger of the previous day. With the weather improving, more sorties were flown and, consequently, there were more opportunities to encounter the Luftwaffe. January 23 proved to be a fruitful day for 122 Wing which claimed 22 aircraft shot down, not counting targets on the ground destroyed or damaged. From this total, 486 contributed two Bf109s destroyed, one Fw190 probably destroyed, and two Fw190s and a Bf109 damaged. The victorious pilots were S/L A.E. Umbers, who was credited with one Bf109 shot down near Rheine, while the second Bf109 was shared between by F/O J.H. Stafford and W/O A.H. Bailey, and a third Bf109 was claimed as damaged by W/O W.J. Campbell around 16.05. On a previous armed recce, which had taken place between 12.20 and 14.05, some Fw190s had been engaged, leading to the probable destruction of a Fw190 in the Minden area by F/O R.J. Danzey, while three more Fw190s had been also claimed as damaged by F/L W.L. Miller and F/O R.D. Bremner.

After close to 200 sorties in January, 486 didn't do much better in February, flying just twenty more, but its scoreboard continued to grow. The first claim was recorded on the 2nd. The day had started badly, however, as, during a morning armed recce, P/O G.J.M. Hooper was shot down while attacking a stationary loco five miles south-west of Nienburg. Hit, he called on the radio to say he was okay and about to attempt a landing, which he did successfully. He was captured the next day. Hooper would eventually manage to escape and evade two months later, crossing the US lines on 19 April. Soon after midday, his loss was balanced with the interception of a Do217 on approach to the airstrip at Paderborn. It was first sighted by Bremner who was followed by Stafford and Sheddan. Bremner opened fire from 800 yards just as the Dornier was touching down. He saw strikes on the wing roots and cockpit, and the Do217 swerved to the left. Bremner pulled up and was able to see flames on the side of the aircraft. The Dornier was finished off by Stafford and Sheddan, coming to a stop and exploding. The claim was shared by the three pilots. The next day, Stafford, helped this time by Eagleson, caught two Ju52s hidden in woods south of Hanover and damaged both. Then, the squadron lost two Tempests in a week, F/L W.L. Miller on the 8th near Verden and Arthur Umbers on the 14th near Meppen. Both were shot down while attacking ground targets, Miller hit by debris, Umbers by flak. Miller was lucky and was rescued by the Dutch resistance, remaining hidden until the Canadians liberated the zone two months later. The CO, sadly, was killed; attacking barges, he was caught under intense rocket flak. His Tempest was immediately boxed in, flicked over on its back and dived directly into the canal in flames. It was a bad day for the Kiwis who had already seen the departure of another pilot, F/O W.A.L. Trott. Also hit by flak, but injured by shrapnel in the lower abdomen, he managed to make it home where he landed his Tempest. He recovered from his wounds but his war was over. A new CO was promoted the next day, Keith Taylor-Cannon, B Flight being taken over by Neville Powell. The second fortnight of the month came down on 486's side. On the 22nd, two Bf109s were shot down near Münster. The two victorious pilots were Stafford and F/O A.R. Evans. Two days later, the new CO and Powell sealed the fate of two others near Bramsche, but the month

Volkel, during the winter of 1944–45, showing Tempests of 486 Sqn taxiing out for their next sortie over Germany.
Below, NV988/SA-Y was shot down on 15 April 1945. The pilot, F/O R.E. Evans, survived. *(KA Smith via P. Sortehaug)*

Keith Granville Tᴀʏʟᴏʀ-Cᴀɴɴᴏɴ
NZ412284

'Hyphen' spent his wartime career with No 486 (NZ) Squadron. He enlisted in the RNZAF in April 1941 and, on completion of training in March 1942, was posted to 486 as an NCO. He made his first claim on 17 December when he destroyed a Bf109. Commissioned, he was awarded a DFC in March 1944 at the end of his first tour. He returned to 486 in August to command B Flight, eventually being promoted to command in February 1945. Soon after, on the 24th, he made his final claim with a Bf109 destroyed over Germany. His tally by then consisted of five confirmed victories (one shared), one shared probable and one V-1. Taylor-Cannon commanded 486 for two months until he was shot down and posted missing on 13 April. He had been awarded a Bar to his DFC the previous month.

Hawker Tempest Mk. V NV986
No. 486 (NZ) Squadron
Squadron Leader KG Taylor-Cannon
B.80/Volkel (Netherlands), March 1945

ended with another loss the next day when W/O RC McPherson experienced engine trouble during an armed recce and made a forced landing in enemy territory. He was captured.

Close to 350 sorties were flown in March, thanks to the weather which made it possible to fly more often. Despite this, there were no encounters with the Luftwaffe. The squadron continued its armed recces and, until the 25th, did not record any loss. That day, F/O W.A. Kalka was hit by small arms fire near Vreden. While he was able to return to base, he was unable to land his Tempest owing to damage sustained to his ailerons. He baled out successfully but came down in the Maas River and drowned. Pilot Officer A.H. Bailey died the next day. He was hit by intense light flak near Gütersloh but made it a good way home, losing height as he went. His engine soon seized but he managed to stretch the glide across the Rhine. He made a forced landing in a field near Wesel but, in the failing light, ploughed into a stone house. A British Army ambulance was promptly on the scene and took him to a nearby hospital, but Bailey died on the way.

By April, German forces were collapsing everywhere. The Allies put on maximum pressure to accelerate the end. Therefore, more sorties were carried out, over 500 for 486. While March was free of any claims, April proved a very productive month with more than thirty made. The first two of the month were claimed by Sheddan on the 6th. In the early evening, he was part of a patrol of four Tempests near the Dümmer See–Steinhuder Meer area when, at around 20.00, they were advised by a forward contact car that Ju87s were attacking the bridge over the Weser at Stolzenau. Guided by AA fire, F/O C.J. Sheddan selected a Ju87 flying at about 4000 feet. He opened fire from 200 yards and closed to almost point-blank range. The Junkers was mortally hit and Sheddan had to manoeuvre violently to the left to avoid ramming it. Two parachutes were seen descending from the Junkers. There was no time to see what happened to them as Sheddan was now after a second dive-bomber which was about a mile from him. An easy prey, Sheddan closed in and opened fire once more from 200 yards, closing with three short bursts to 100 yards, but initially seeing no strikes. He pulled out to the left and made a further attack from the right. While positioning for a fourth attack, he saw a parachute open and the Ju87 commence a gliding turn. It spiralled slowly toward the ground and, soon after a second parachute opened, crashed and blew up. Four days later, in the evening during an armed recce, F/L W.E. Schrader claimed a Fw190 flying alone with long-range tanks at 8000 feet near Nienburg. This would be the last claim made from Volkel, the squadron moving to B.118/Hapsten in Germany two days later. Having been there for just a couple of hours, patrols and armed recces resumed and it was not long before another claim was made, this time by F/L J.H. Stafford who claimed a Fw190 destroyed east of Ludwigslust late in the evening. These claims were rapidly balanced by the loss of the CO and F/Sgt W.J.K. Hart. Having taken off on a late morning patrol to strafe motorised transport near Dömitz, almost over the bridge itself, the Tempest flown by S/L Taylor-Cannon was seen to suffer a direct hit from an 88 shell and catch fire. He baled out and was seen to land safely. Everyone could only hope he became a PoW, but no trace of him was ever found. What happened to him remains a mystery, but it is likely he was killed soon after he reached the ground. Neither his body nor his gravesite have been found. In the afternoon, Hart was in trouble. After having strafed METs and a loco, the patrol returned to base, but Hart's engine failed and he was forced to land at high speed in a small

Tempest NV986/SA-F (S/L Taylor-Cannon' regular mount) about to start its engine in March 1945; a lucky photo as this aircraft only served three weeks that month as it was sent out for repairs after P/O Melles damaged the mainplane flying too low over the Dümmer See area.

Some of 486 Squadron's pilots after an op in March 1945. Left to right: Flying Officers O.D. Eagleson and D.J. Thomson, S/L K.G. Taylor-Cannon (CO, †17.04.45), F/O R.J. Danzey, W/O W.J. Shaw, F/L J.H. Stafford, and Flying Officers K.A. Smith (PoW 26.04.45), R.D. Bremner, C.J. MacDonald and A.R. Evans. All but Thomson and Shaw were awarded the DFC while serving with 486. *(KA Smith via P. Sortehaug)*

paddock near Rheine in British-held territory; things went wrong and he was badly injured in the process. He was recovered and spent the next few weeks in hospital before returning to the squadron in July; the war was over. The Kiwis got soon their revenge. The very next day, Sheddan shot down an Fw190 north of Ludwigslust in the middle of the afternoon and, in the evening, W/O W.J. Shaw claimed another while F/O S.J. Short claimed a Bf109 as damaged in the same area. The action started when the Tempests were caught by surprise while strafing along the rail tracks near Ludwigslust. Warrant Officer O.J. Mitchell was shot down and killed but Shaw managed to reverse the situation by sealing the fate of a 190 in one long burst. It could be strange to claim two types of aircraft in a single engagement, but the fact was that the Kiwis had engaged the new Ta152 which could be mistaken for a Bf109. The next day, only one patrol was flown but it would prove to be the most productive ever for 486. The squadron got airborne at 08.30 for an armed recce of the Müritzee Lake area. A formation of Fw190s was sighted a few miles south-east of Uelzen; when first seen, the Germans were to the right of 486 and flying a reciprocal course. Led by F/L Schrader, the Kiwis gave chase. At about 1000 yards, the Fw190s scattered and each member of the patrol selected a target. Schrader chose the aircraft on the extreme left of the formation and caught it during its turn. He fired from 300 yards and the Fw190 was immediately hit; having seen some pieces shedding from the aircraft, Schrader watched as it burst into flames, rolled on to its back and spiralled down in an almost vertical attitude. Joining the general melee, he soon sealed the fate of another Fw190. Schrader's wingman, W/O R.J. Atkinson got one more with a short burst that hit the cockpit. The Fw190 caught fire, then the nose dropped and the fighter was seen to plunge in flames into the middle of a forest. Flying Officer B.J. O'Connor claimed an Fw190 destroyed and one more damaged, while F/L A.I. Ross, F/O A.R. Evans, W/O G. Maddaford and F/Sgt R.A. Melles each claimed a Fw190 destroyed. It was an impressive score for the loss of just one Tempest; Evans was shot down but managed to bale out, rejoining the squadron later that day. The next day, the 16th, 486 continued to score, with an Fw190 destroyed near Neustadt in the morning, shared by Sheddan and Shaw, and, in the afternoon, Schrader and F/O J.W. Reid each claimed an Fw190 destroyed near Ludwigslust. Schrader was again in the headlines a few days later when, on the 21st, he was promoted to squadron leader to take command of 486. His A Flight CO position was assumed by Sheddan. It was in this new position that Schrader made his next claim. Operating near the Parchim–Schwerin area, he and Evans caught two Bf109s preparing to land at Schwerin airfield. One of the Bf109s already had its wheels down and was flying slowly, making it easy prey. However, Schrader opened fire from half a mile to deter the pilot from landing. The German understood the message and pulled up into a tight climbing turn, attempting to escape his fate. Schrader had already closed in and fired from close range. The Bf109 continued to turn and, in a shallow dive, barely a mile to the south of the airfield, hit the ground, bounced back into the air and flipped over on its back before coming to rest. The aircraft had broken into several pieces but had not caught fire so Schrader and his No. 2 strafed it until it burned. Soon after, Evans spied a Fw190 heading towards Wismar airfield. He shot it down with a single burst from 300 yards. This impressive series of claims was cooled by the loss of F/Sgt W.W. May on the 24th when he was shot down by flak while attacking ground targets near Hamburg. Fortunately, although badly injured, he was captured.

Warren Edward Schrader

NZ411944

'Smoky' Schrader joined the RNZAF in March 1941. Following training in New Zealand, Canada and the UK, he was posted as an NCO to 165 Sqn in April 1942. He was commissioned and remained with the squadron until the end of the year. During February 1943, he left for an overseas posting and, by March, was serving with 1435 Sqn, operating Spitfires, on Malta, later moving with the unit to Italy. He had been appointed a flight commander, during July while on Malta, but it wasn't until being based in Italy that he made his first claims. In November, he destroyed an Italian bomber on the ground and, on 17 December, scored a double kill by shooting down two Bf109s. He shared in shooting down another fighter on 3 January 1944 and was awarded the DFC in April, his tour ending the following month. He was rested and served as a flying instructor until returning to the UK at the beginning of 1945. He transitioned to the Hawker Typhoon and Tempest and joined 486 in March, taking over the squadron in April, succeeding S/L Taylor-Cannon. That month was to be a very successful one with Schrader making nine claims in three weeks. On 1 May, he scored his last aerial victory, a Bf109, to bring his total to thirteen confirmed victories (two shared). The next day, he was promoted to wing commander and given command of 616 (South Yorkshire) Squadron to fly Gloster Meteor jets. In the week preceding VE-Day, he managed to destroy three German aircraft on the ground. He was awarded a Bar to his DFC, left 616 Sqn in August, and the RNZAF in December 1946.

Hawker Tempest Mk. V NV969
No. 486 (NZ) Squadron
Squadron Leader WE Schrader
B.80/Volkel (Netherlands), April 1945

Four days later, F/O K.A. Smith distinguished himself by claiming an Me262 destroyed, the first jet claimed by the squadron since Stafford and Bremner's success the previous December. He got lucky when, during a patrol, he spotted two Me262s. He managed, with his wingman, to trail the two jets back to their airfield at Lübeck and caught one of them in the circuit. He was able to deliver two attacks and, when he left the scene, could see the jet had careered off the runway and that smoke and flames appeared to be coming from it. He didn't have time to celebrate much as, the following day, he was shot down by flak north of Uithiele while attacking METs. Damaged, he headed for home but was obliged to make a forced landing in a paddock near Hamburg. Smith was taken prisoner soon after and put in a prison cell in Hamburg itself. He was joined by Melles who was also shot down by flak in the area the next day. Their captivity was brief as they both escaped together and rejoined the squadron on 5 May. In the meantime, the unit had made another move and was now at B.150/Fassberg in Germany. On the 28th, late in the afternoon west of Plon, F/L J.W. Reid and F/O O.D. Eagleson claimed an aircraft they identified as a Ju352; the claim was confirmed but Intelligence altered the claim to a Ju52 after viewing the gun camera films. Both pilots remained convinced the aircraft they had attacked had been much larger than the ubiquitous Ju52. On the 29th, the Elbe, the last barrier facing the 21st Army Group before they met the Soviets, was crossed with relative ease at Lauenberg. Many patrols were flown to cover the bridgehead during the day. The Luftwaffe was at the rendezvous and many encounters occurred. Not much after midday, the first claim was made by the CO when he destroyed an Fw190. Ten minutes later, more hostile aircraft appeared, leading to a major dogfight which ended with two more Bf109s credited to Schrader (making three confirmed kills for him for the day), a third Bf109 shared with W/O N.D. Howard (who also claimed another as damaged), while Eagleson was good for one Fw190 destroyed and a second damaged, one Fw190 destroyed for F/O C.S. Kennedy and another probably destroyed by Evans. The squadron returned to the same area in the middle of the afternoon and another combat took place with the Luftwaffe; three more Fw190s were shot down, one each credited to Reid, F/O C.J. McDonald and W/O J.R. Duncan. That evening, during the last patrol of the day, Evans claimed a tenth victory for 486, his victim being a Bf109 which fell two miles south of Bergedorf. The month ended with another claim, a Bf109 claimed as damaged near Ludwigslust.

Even with the war in Europe approaching its inevitable end, the rhythm of operations was maintained during the first days of May. More than 100 sorties were flown and activity remained intense. On 1 May, Schrader claimed a Bf109 shot down over Bad Segeberg, while, the next day, Eagleson, during the first armed recce of the day, saw an Fw44 flying on the deck seven miles south of Schwerin; he attacked and easily shot it down, the aircraft crashing in flames. The same pilot, during the next armed recce, saw an Fi156 on the ground and destroyed it as well. His luck eventually left him later in the evening when he was hit by flak while attacking a stationary train near Lübeck. Eagleson made an emergency landing in enemy territory but managed to escape capture and was back with the squadron two days later. He had made a good landing unscathed and was actually captured by German soldiers soon after. He escaped during a halt while retreating from British forces. In the meantime, during a previous armed recce, P/O W.J. Shaw and W/O N.D. Howard shared in the destruction of an Fi156 and a Fw190 south of Neumünster. The day was not over, however, as, very late in the evening, a final claim was made by Sheddan and F/O D.J. Thompson. Sheddan had just been promoted to lead 486 earlier in the day after Schrader was posted to command No. 616 Squadron, the first jet squadron in the RAF. Now Squadron Leader Sheddan was leading the formation for the last armed recce of the day in the Fulda area. Suddenly, he saw a German flying boat

The squadron's Tempests dispersed at Fassberg just before leaving for Kastrup in Denmark via Celle. *(JM Williams via P. Sortehaug)*

orbiting; he identified it as a multi-engine (possibly a Bv139) aircraft and attacked it from astern. He saw various strikes on the fuselage and the two right engines. Both engines streamed smoke and the flying boat lost height and landed on the water, swinging onto the beach. By this time, it had caught fire and was last seen with several explosions spreading debris across the beach. As Thompson had participated in the attack, the claim was shared. The last enemy aircraft to fall to 486's guns were two Ju88s shot down north-west of Jagel, the two victorious pilots being MacDonald and Duncan. May 3 was also a bad day for 486 as two Tempests were lost. The first was flown by P/O J.E. Wood; hit by flak, he had to put his Tempest down north-west of Neumünster. He was apprehended by a civilian who locked him up in a lavatory, but he managed to escape and rejoined the squadron ten days later. By that time, the war was over. In the late afternoon, it was the turn of F/O C.E. Blee to be shot down, being caught by flak over Hamburg while returning home. While he made a crash landing in a friendly sector, he suffered bad fractures in his back, skull and arm in the process. He would need a full year to recover before he was repatriated to New Zealand. These two pilots were not the squadron's last losses of the war. The next day, F/O T.M. Austin experienced engine trouble while attacking a Fi156 with several other pilots. While the Fi156 was finally destroyed on the ground, Austin was obliged to make a belly landing in an enemy-held sector and was immediately captured and taken to hospital with a broken wrist. He was eventually released on 10 May. The next day, the 5th, 486 carried out its last sorties of the war, an escort for Dakotas carrying Military Mission personnel to Copenhagen. Led by Sheddan, the escort took place between 17.15 and 19.45 and was completed without incident. Over the next few days, 486 made two moves: B.118/Celle in Germany on the 6th and B.160/Karup in Denmark two days later. Another move followed on 6 July, the squadron returning to Germany to be stationed at B.158/Lubeck until disbandment was announced on 7 September 1945. During this period of peace and rest, the squadron continued to fly many practice sorties. Some ended badly, like on 19 June when a wing panel flew off Eagleson's aircraft. He baled out into Copenhagen harbour and was rescued unscathed. Two months later, and two weeks before disbandment, P/O W.J. Shaw hit the sea while flying too low; while he managed to return to base, he crashed his Tempest and fractured his spine. His aircraft was not repaired and was struck off charge the following October.

Some of 486 Sqn in front of an Fw190 at Kastrup airfield near Copenhagen. The photograph was taken on 9 May 1945 by a photographer from the Danish daily paper Politiken.
Standing, left to right: F/L F.P. Kendall (British), F/Sgt J.W. Reid, W/O N.D. Howard, F/Sgt R.D. Roderick, W/O R.J. Atkinson, F/O C.J. MacDonald, P/O W.J. Shaw, W/O G. Maddaford, F/L B.S. Griffiths (British) and W/O R. Bird (British).
Squatting, left to right: F/Sgt R.A. Melles (†29.08.45 in a car accident), P/O H.T. Leach (British), F/O D.J. Thomson and F/L A.I. Ross. In the final weeks of the war, the lack of Kiwi pilots trained on Tempests obliged 2TAF to post in Australian and British pilots to replace losses and tour-expired departures.
(Melles family via P. Sortehaug)

Date	Pilot	SN	Origin	Type	Serial	Code	Nb	Cat.
16.06.44	F/Sgt Brian J. **O'Connor**	NZ402747	RNZAF	*V-1*	**JN809**	SA-M	1.0	C
	P/O Kevin **McCarthy**	NZ417075	RNZAF	*V-1*	**JN801**	SA-L	1.0	C
17.06.44	F/O Thomas M. **Fenton**	NZ422273	RNZAF	*V-1*	**JN808**	SA-N	1.0	C
	P/O Raymond J. **Danzey**	NZ416464	RNZAF	*V-1*	**JN809**	SA-M	1.0	C
	N.B: 150 Wing ORB gives 4 V-1s destroyed for 486 that day.							
18.06.44	F/O William A. **Hart**	NZ424461	RNZAF	*V-1*	**JN797**	SA-K	1.0	C
	F/O Neville J. **Powell**	NZ415013	RNZAF	*V-1*	**JN804**	SA-R	1.0	C
	F/Sgt Owen D. **Eagleson**	NZ421689	RNZAF	*V-1*	**JN811**	SA-Z	1.0	C
	P/O Raymond J. **Danzey**	NZ416464	RNZAF	*V-1*	**JN797**	SA-K	1.0	C
	F/O James G. **Wilson**	NZ403555	RNZAF	*V-1*	**JN809**	SA-M	1.0	C
	F/L Vaughan St.C. **Cooke**	NZ404898	RNZAF	*V-1*	**JN801**	SA-L	1.0	C
	F/Sgt Owen D. **Eagleson**	NZ421689	RNZAF	*V-1*	**JN804**	SA-R	2.0	C
	F/Sgt Bevan M. **Hall**	NZ421705	RNZAF	*V-1*	**JN809**	SA-M	1.0	C
	F/Sgt Roland J. **Wright**	NZ421131	RNZAF	*V-1*	**JN770**	SA-V	1.0	C
	F/O James R. **Cullen**	NZ416462	RNZAF	*V-1*	**JN758**	SA-Y	1.0	C
	F/O Stamford S. **Williams**	NZ412297	RNZAF	*V-1*	**JN810**	SA-P	1.0	C
19.06.44	F/O William L. **Miller**	NZ402208	RNZAF	*V-1*	**JN811**	SA-Z	1.0	C
	F/O Raymond J. **Cammock**	NZ414723	RNZAF	*V-1*	**JN810**	SA-P	1.0	C
	F/Sgt John H. **Stafford**	NZ421783	RNZAF	*V-1*	**JN803**	SA-D	1.0	C
	F/L Harvey N. **Sweetman**	NZ40992	RNZAF	*V-1*	**JN754**	SA-A	1.0	C
	F/L James H. **McCaw**	NZ414311	RNZAF	*V-1*	**JN770**	SA-V	1.0	C
20.06.44	P/O Raymond J. **Danzey**	NZ416464	RNZAF	*V-1*	**JN801**	SA-L	1.0	C
	F/Sgt John H. **Stafford**	NZ421783	RNZAF	*V-1*	**JN808**	SA-N	1.0	C
	F/L James H. **McCaw**	NZ414311	RNZAF	*V-1*	**JN758**	SA-Y	1.0	C
21.06.44	F/O Stamford S. **Williams***	NZ412297	RNZAF	*V-1*	**JN866**	SA-U	1.0	C
	N.B: 150 Wing ORB gives 3 V-1s destroyed for 486 that day.							
22.06.44	F/L James H. **McCaw**	NZ414311	RNZAF	*V-1*	**JN758**	SA-Y	1.0	C
				V-1	**JN808**	SA-N	1.0	C
	P/O Kevin **McCarthy**	NZ417075	RNZAF	*V-1*	**JN801**	SA-L	2.0	C
	F/O William L. **Miller**	NZ402208	RNZAF	*V-1*	**JN794**	SA-T	1.0	C
	W/O Garnet J. **Hooper**	NZ431213	RNZAF	*V-1*	**JN809**	SA-M	0.33	C
	Shared with two Spitfires, possibly of 91 Sqn							
	F/L James H. **McCaw**	NZ414311	RNZAF	*V-1*	**JN821**	SA-H	1.0	C
	W/O Cornelius J. **Sheddan**	NZ412358	RNZAF	*V-1*	**JN809**	SA-M	1.0	C
	S/L James H. **Iremonger**	RAF No. 33342	RAF	*V-1*	**JN808**	SA-N	1.0	C
	F/Sgt John H. **Stafford**	NZ421783	RNZAF	*V-1*	**JN803**	SA-D	1.0	C
23.06.44	P/O Raymond J. **Danzey**	NZ416464	RNZAF	*V-1*	**JN797**	SA-K	1.50	C
	Second claim shared with a Tempest of 3 Sqn							
	P/O Frank B. **Lawless**	NZ411417	RNZAF	*V-1*	**JN859**	SA-S	1.0	C
	F/Sgt Bevan M. **Hall**	NZ421705	RNZAF	*V-1*	**JN809**	SA-M	1.0	C
	P/O Kevin **McCarthy**	NZ417075	RNZAF	*V-1*	**JN754**	SA-A	2.0	C
	F/Sgt Owen D. **Eagleson**	NZ421689	RNZAF	*V-1*	**JN794**	SA-T	1.0	C
	F/O William L. **Miller**	NZ402208	RNZAF	*V-1*	**JN808**	SA-N	2.0	C
	F/O Raymond J. **Cammock**	NZ414723	RNZAF	*V-1*	**JN810**	SA-P	0.5	C
	Shared with a Spitfire of 91 Sqn							
	W/O Cornelius J. **Sheddan**	NZ412358	RNZAF	*V-1*	**JN801**	SA-L	1.0	C
	F/Sgt Sydney J. **Short**	NZ42465	RNZAF	*V-1*	**JN810**	SA-P	1.0	C
	F/Sgt Owen D. **Eagleson**	NZ421689	RNZAF	*V-1*	**JN794**	SA-T	0.5	C
	Shared with a Spitfire of 41 Sqn							
	F/O James R. **Cullen**	NZ416462	RNZAF	*V-1*	**JN770**	SA-V	0.5	C
	Claim shared with a Tempest of 3 Sqn							

Date	Name	Serial No.	Service	Type	Aircraft	Code	Score	
	W/O William A. **Kalka***	NZ415415	RNZAF	*V-1*	**JN801**	SA-L	1.0	C
	F/O Raymond J. **Cammock**	NZ414723	RNZAF	*V-1*	**JN810**	SA-P	1.0	C
24.06.44	F/O Raymond J. **Cammock**	NZ414723	RNZAF	*V-1*	**JN808**	SA-N	2.0	C
	P/O Kevin **McCarthy**	NZ417075	RNZAF	*V-1*	**JN803**	SA-D	1.0	C
	N.B: 150 Wing ORB gives 5 V-1s destroyed for 486 that day.							
25.06.44	F/O Stamford S. **Williams**	NZ412297	RNZAF	*V-1*	**JN758**	SA-Y	1.0	C
	F/Sgt Sydney J. **Short**	NZ42465	RNZAF	*V-1*	**JN801**	SA-P	1.0	C
	F/O Raymond J. **Cammock**	NZ414723	RNZAF	*V-1*	**JN804**	SA-R	1.0	C
	F/O James R. **Cullen**	NZ416462	RNZAF	*V-1*	**JN770**	SA-V	2.0	C
	W/O Cornelius J. **Sheddan**	NZ412358	RNZAF	*V-1*	**JN854**	SA-G	1.0	C
	F/O Raymond J. **Cammock**	NZ414723	RNZAF	*V-1*	**JN804**	SA-R	1.0	C
	F/O William A. **Hart**	NZ424461	RNZAF	*V-1*	**JN809**	SA-M	1.0	C
26.06.44	F/L James H. **McCaw**	NZ414311	RNZAF	*V-1*	**JN758**	SA-Y	1.0	C
	N.B: 150 Wing ORB gives 4 V-1s destroyed for 486 that day.							
27.06.44	F/O Neville J. **Powell**	NZ415013	RNZAF	*V-1*	**JN866**	SA-U	1.0	C
	W/O John R. **Powell**	NZ413889	RNZAF	*V-1*	**JN866**	SA-U	1.0	C
	F/L Harvey N. **Sweetman**	NZ40992	RNZAF	*V-1*	**JN754**	SA-A	1.0	C
				V-1	**JN821**	SA-H	1.0	C
	W/O Garnet J. **Hooper**	NZ431213	RNZAF	*V-1*	**JN803**	SA-D	2.0	C
	F/O William L. **Miller**	NZ402208	RNZAF	*V-1*	**JN811**	SA-Z	1.0	C
	W/O Owen D. **Eagleson**	NZ421689	RNZAF	*V-1*	**JN794**	SA-T	0.5	C
	Shared with a Tempest of 3 Sqn							
	F/O William A. **Hart**	NZ424461	RNZAF	*V-1*	**JN803**	SA-D	1.0	C
	F/O Raymond J. **Cammock**	NZ414723	RNZAF	*V-1*	**JN794**	SA-T	1.0	C
28.06.44	F/O James G. **Wilson**	NZ403555	RNZAF	*V-1*	**JN866**	SA-U	1.0	C
	W/O Owen D. **Eagleson**	NZ421689	RNZAF	*V-1*	**JN859**	SA-S	1.0	C
				V-1	**JN854**	SA-G	1.0	C
	F/O Raymond J. **Cammock**	NZ414723	RNZAF	*V-1*	**JN810**	SA-P	1.0	C
	P/O Frank B. **Lawless***	NZ411417	RNZAF	*V-1*	**JN859**	SA-S	1.0	C
	F/Sgt Bevan M. **Hall***	NZ421705	RNZAF	*V-1*	**JN809**	SA-M	1.0	C
	F/Sgt Roland J. **Wright***	NZ421131	RNZAF	*V-1*	**JN804**	SA-R	1.0	C
	N.B: 150 Wing ORB gives 5 V-1s destroyed for 486 that day.							
29.06.44	P/O Raymond J. **Danzey**	NZ416464	RNZAF	*V-1*	**JN797**	SA-K	2.0	C
	P/O Robert D. **Bremmer**	NZ424417	RNZAF	*V-1*	**JN821**	SA-H	1.0	C
	F/L Harvey N. **Sweetman**	NZ40992	RNZAF	*V-1*	**JN821**	SA-H	1.0	C
	F/Sgt John **Steedman**	NZ422328	RNZAF	V-1	**JN821**	SA-H	1.0	C
	W/O Cornelius J. **Sheddan**	NZ412358	RNZAF	*V-1*	**JN809**	SA-M	1.0	C
	W/O Sydney J. **Short**	NZ42465	RNZAF	*V-1*	**EJ527**	SA-Q	2.0	C
	F/O James R. **Cullen**	NZ416462	RNZAF	*V-1*	**JN810**	SA-P	1.0	C
30.06.44	W/O Sydney J. **Short**	NZ42465	RNZAF	*V-1*	**JN810**	SA-P	1.0	C
	F/Sgt Bevan M. **Hall**	NZ421705	RNZAF	*V-1*	**JN821**	SA-H	1.0	C
	P/O Frank B. **Lawless**	NZ411417	RNZAF	*V-1*	**JN811**	SA-Z	1.0	C
	F/L Eric W. **Tanner**	NZ415037	RNZAF	*V-1*	**JN770**	SA-V	3.0	C
	W/O John H. **Stafford**	NZ421783	RNZAF	*V-1*	**JN801**	SA-L	1.0	C
	F/Sgt Bevan M. **Hall**	NZ421705	RNZAF	*V-1*	**JN854**	SA-G	1.0	C
	F/L Harvey N. **Sweetman***	NZ40992	RNZAF	*V-1*	**JN801**	SA-L	1.0	C
	N.B: 150 Wing ORB gives 10 V-1s destroyed for 486 that day.							
01.07.44	P/O Frank B. **Lawless**	NZ411417	RNZAF	*V-1*	**JN770**	SA-V	1.0	C
	F/O Raymond J. **Cammock**	NZ414723	RNZAF	*V-1*	**JN866**	SA-U	1.0	C
	W/O Cornelius J. **Sheddan**	NZ412358	RNZAF	*V-1*	**JN821**	SA-H	1.0	C
	F/L Lloyd J. **Appleton**	NZ415213	RNZAF	*V-1*	**JN873**	SA-W	1.0	C
03.07.44	P/O Robert D. **Bremmer**	NZ424417	RNZAF	*V-1*	**JN801**	SA-L	1.0	C
	F/O James R. **Cullen**	NZ416462	RNZAF	*V-1*	**JN863**	SA-R	1.0	C
	W/O Owen D. **Eagleson**	NZ421689	RNZAF	*V-1*	**JN873**	SA-W	1.0	C
	P/O Keith A. **Smith**	NZ403828	RNZAF	*V-1*	**JN801**	SA-L	2.0	C
	W/O Cornelius J. **Sheddan**	NZ412358	RNZAF	*V-1*	**JN805**	SA-E	1.0	C
04.07.44	F/O Henry M. **Mason**	NZ413104	RNZAF	*V-1*	**JN805**	SA-E	1.0	C
	F/O James R. **Cullen**	NZ416462	RNZAF	*V-1*	**JN770**	SA-V	1.0	C

Some of the squadron's V-1 experts:
Above left, F/O R.J. Cammock. Before being posted to 486 Sqn in May 1944, he completed a tour with 485 and 253 Squadrons, initially in the UK and then in North Africa, returning to the UK in July 1943. He was killed in action on 6 October 1944. *(Cammock family via P. Sortehaug)*
Above right, F/O R.J. Danzey was posted to 486 as an NCO. He left in March 1945, tour-expired, and survived the war. *(R.J. Danzay via P. Sortheaug)*
Below, R.J. Cammock (right) chatting with W/O O.D. Eagleson. The latter arrived at 486 in November 1943 for flying duties and would remain with the squadron almost until the end of war. He was captured on 2 May 1945, evaded the next day, was recaptured later that day, and escaped again on the 4th!
(via P. Sortehaug)

Date	Name	Service No.	Force		Aircraft	Code	Score	
	W/O Owen D. **Eagleson**	NZ421689	RNZAF	*V-1*	**EJ537**	SA-S	1.0	C
	W/O William A. **Kalka**	NZ415415	RNZAF	*V-1*	**JN809**	SA-M	2.0	C
	P/O Frank B. **Lawless**	NZ411417	RNZAF	*V-1*	**EJ537**	SA-S	1.0	C
	F/L Harvey N. **Sweetman**	NZ40992	RNZAF	*V-1*	**JN809**	SA-M	1.0	C
	P/O Robert D. **Bremmer**	NZ424417	RNZAF	*V-1*	**JN854**	SA-G	1.0	C
	F/O Neville J. **Powell**	NZ415013	RNZAF	*V-1*	**EJ527**	SA-Q	1.0	C
	W/O John H. **Stafford**	NZ421783	RNZAF	*V-1*	**JN854**	SA-G	2.0	C
	F/O Stamford S. **Williams***	NZ412297	RNZAF	*V-1*	**JN820**	SA-P	1.0	C
	F/O Henry M. **Mason**	NZ413104	RNZAF	*V-1*	**JN809**	SA-M	0.5	C
	Possibly shared with a Tempest of 56 Sqn							
	P/O Raymond J. **Danzey**	NZ416464	RNZAF	*V-1*	**JN805**	SA-E	1.0	C
05.07.44	W/O Cornelius J. **Sheddan**	NZ412358	RNZAF	*V-1*	**JN854**	SA-G	1.0	C
	W/C Roland P. **Beamont**	RAF No. 41819	RAF	*V-1*	**JN751**	R-P	1.0	C
	F/Sgt Brian J. **O'Connor**	NZ402747	RNZAF	*V-1*	**JN803**	SA-D	1.0	C
06.07.44	F/Sgt Brian J. **O'Connor**	NZ402747	RNZAF	*V-1*	**JN803**	SA-D	1.5	C
	Shared with a Tempest of 3 Sqn							
	W/O Owen D. **Eagleson**	NZ421689	RNZAF	*V-1*	**JN873**	SA-W	1.0	C
	W/O Garnet J. **Hooper**	NZ431213	RNZAF	*V-1*	**JN805**	SA-E	2.5	C
	Third claim shared with a Tempest of 3 Sqn							
07.07.44	F/L Harvey N. **Sweetman**	NZ40992	RNZAF	*V-1*	**JN801**	SA-L	0.5	C
	P/O Raymond J. **Danzey**	NZ416464	RNZAF		**JN809**	SA-M	0.5	C
	F/L Harvey N. **Sweetman**	NZ40992	RNZAF	*V-1*	**JN803**	SA-D	1.0	C
	W/O Owen D. **Eagleson**	NZ421689	RNZAF	*V-1*	**EJ527**	SA-Q	1.0	C
	F/O Raymond J. **Cammock**	NZ414723	RNZAF	*V-1*	**JN873**	SA-W	1.0	C
	F/O James R. **Cullen**	NZ416462	RNZAF	*V-1*	**EJ527**	SA-Q	1.0	C
	F/O Henry M. **Mason***	NZ413104	RNZAF	*V-1*	**JN732**	SA-I	1.0	C
	W/O Owen D. **Eagleson**	NZ421689	RNZAF	*V-1*	**JN873**	SA-W	1.0	C
08.07.44	F/O James R. **Cullen**	NZ416462	RNZAF	*V-1*	**JN770**	SA-V	1.0	C
	F/L James H. **McCaw**	NZ414311	RNZAF	*V-1*	**JN758**	SA-Y	4.0	C
	P/O Frank B. **Lawless**	NZ411417	RNZAF	*V-1*	**JN770**	SA-Y	2.0	C
09.07.44	F/O James R. **Cullen**	NZ416462	RNZAF	*V-1*	**JN873**	SA-W	1.5	C
	Shared with a Tempest of 56 Sqn							
	W/O Garnet J. **Hooper**	NZ431213	RNZAF	*V-1*	**JN821**	SA-H	2.0	C
11.07.44	*The claims made by 486 that day were not confirmed*							
12.07.44	W/O Owen D. **Eagleson***	NZ421689	RNZAF	*V-1*	**EJ527**	SA-Q	1.0	C
	P/O Bevan M. **Hall**	NZ421705	RNZAF	*V-1*	**JN805**	SA-E	0.5	C
	Shared with a Tempest of 3 Sqn							
	F/L James H. **McCaw***	NZ414311	RNZAF	*V-1*	**JN770**	SA-V	1.0	C
	F/O Stamford S. **Williams**	NZ412297	RNZAF	*V-1*	**EN523**	SA-X	1.0	C
	P/O Bevan M. **Hall**	NZ421705	RNZAF	*V-1*	**JN821**	SA-H	1.0	C
	W/O William A. **Kalka**	NZ415415	RNZAF	*V-1*	**JN803**	SA-D	4.0	C
	F/Sgt James S. **Ferguson**	RAF No. 1558633	RAF	*V-1*	**JN767**	SA-B	1.0	C
	F/L Lloyd J. **Appleton***	NZ415213	RNZAF	*V-1*	**JN770**	SA-V	0.5	C
	shared with ???							
	F/L Eric W. **Tanner***	NZ415037	RNZAF	*V-1*	**EN528**	SA-P	0.5	C
	shared with ???							
13.07.44	F/O Henry M. **Mason**	NZ413104	RNZAF	*V-1*	**JN732**	SA-I	2.0	C
	P/O William A.L. **Trott**	NZ417131	RNZAF	*V-1*	**JN866**	SA-U	1.0	C
	W/O Brian J. **O'Connor**	NZ402747	RNZAF	*V-1*	**JN866**	SA-U	1.0	C
14.07.44	F/L James H. **McCaw**	NZ414311	RNZAF	*V-1*	**JN758**	SA-Y	2.0	C
	W/O Owen D. **Eagleson**	NZ421689	RNZAF	*V-1*	**EN523**	SA-X	1.0	C
	F/O Stamford S. **Williams**	NZ412297	RNZAF	*V-1*	**JN860**	SA-Z	1.0	C
	F/O Henry M. **Mason**	NZ413104	RNZAF	*V-1*	**JN732**	SA-I	0.5	C
	Shared with a Tempest of 56 Sqn							
	F/O James R. **Cullen**	NZ416462	RNZAF	*V-1*	**JN770**	SA-V	1.0	C
15.07.44	F/L James H. **McCaw**	NZ414311	RNZAF	*V-1*	**JN860**	SA-Z	1.0	C
	W/O Garnet J. **Hooper**	NZ431213	RNZAF	*V-1*	**JN803**	SA-D	1.0	C

Date	Pilot	Serial	Service	Target	Aircraft	Code	Score	
16.07.44	P/O Bevan M. **HALL**	NZ421705	RNZAF	*V-1*	**JN821**	SA-H	0.5	C
	Shared with a Tempest of 3 Sqn							
	P/O Raymond J. **DANZEY**	NZ416464	RNZAF	*V-1*	**JN803**	SA-D	1.0	C
18.07.44	S/L James H. **IREMONGER**	RAF No. 33342	RAF	*V-1*	**JN763**	SA-F	0.5	C
	F/O James R. **CULLEN**	NZ416462	RNZAF	*V-1*	**JN770**	SA-V	0.5	C
	F/L Harvey N. **SWEETMAN**	NZ40992	RNZAF	*V-1*	**JN754**	SA-A	1.0	C
	F/O James R. **CULLEN**	NZ416462	RNZAF	*V-1*	**JN770**	SA-V	0.5	C
	Shared with a Tempest of 56 Sqn							
19.07.44	F/O Stamford S. **WILLIAMS**	NZ412297	RNZAF	*V-1*	**EJ523**	SA-X	1.0	C
20.07.44	P/O Robert D. **BREMMER**	NZ424417	RNZAF	*V-1*	**JN802**	SA-C	0.5	C
	W/O Garnet J. **HOOPER**	NZ431213	RNZAF	*V-1*	**JN797**	SA-K	0.5	C
21.07.44	F/L James H. **McCAW**	NZ414311	RNZAF	*V-1*	**JN758**	SA-Y	1.0	C
22.07.44	F/O Raymond J. **CAMMOCK**	NZ414723	RNZAF	*V-1*	**JN863**	SA-R	1.0	C
	F/O James R. **CULLEN**	NZ416462	RNZAF	*V-1*	**EJ537**	SA-S	1.0	C
	P/O Raymond J. **DANZEY**	NZ416464	RNZAF	*V-1*	**JN801**	SA-L	1.0	C
	F/O James R. **CULLEN**	NZ416462	RNZAF	*V-1*	**EJ523**	SA-X	1.0	C
23.07.44	P/O William A.L. **TROTT**	NZ417131	RNZAF	*V-1*	**JN758**	SA-Y	2.0	C
24.07.44	F/L Lloyd J. **APPLETON**	NZ415213	RNZAF	*V-1*	**JN863**	SA-R	1.0	C
	F/L Eric W. **TANNER**	NZ415037	RNZAF	*V-1*	**JN732**	SA-I	1.0	C
26.07.44	P/O Robert D. **BREMMER**	NZ424417	RNZAF	*V-1*	**JN803**	SA-D	1.0	C
	F/O William A. **HART**	NZ424461	RNZAF	*V-1*	**JN732**	SA-I	1.0	C
	F/O Raymond J. **CAMMOCK**	NZ414723	RNZAF	*V-1*	**EJ523**	SA-X	1.0	C
	F/L James H. **McCAW**	NZ414311	RNZAF	*V-1*	**JN770**	SA-V	1.0	C
	P/O Keith A. **SMITH**	NZ403828	RNZAF	*V-1*	**JN803**	SA-D	1.0	C
	F/L Vaughan St.C. **COOKE**	NZ404898	RNZAF	*V-1*	**JN763**	SA-F	0.5	C
	Shared with a Tempest of 3 Sqn							
	F/O Raymond J. **CAMMOCK**	NZ414723	RNZAF	*V-1*	**JN770**	SA-V	1.0	C
	F/O James R. **CULLEN**	NZ416462	RNZAF	*V-1*	**JN770**	SA-V	1.0	C
	W/O John H. **STAFFORD**	NZ421783	RNZAF	*V-1*	**JN803**	SA-D	1.0	C
27.07.44	F/O William A. **HART**	NZ424461	RNZAF	*V-1*	**JN754**	SA-A	0.5	C
	P/O Robert D. **BREMMER**	NZ424417	RNZAF		**JN803**	SA-D	0.5	C
	P/O William A.L. **TROTT**	NZ417131	RNZAF	*V-1*	**JN763**	SA-F	1.0	C
	F/O Raymond J. **CAMMOCK**	NZ414723	RNZAF	*V-1*	**EJ523**	SA-X	2.0	C
	F/L James H. **McCAW**	NZ414311	RNZAF	*V-1*	**JN770**	SA-V	1.0	C
	W/O Owen D. **EAGLESON**	NZ421689	RNZAF	*V-1*	**EJ586**	SA-Z	1.0	C
	W/O Brian J. **O'CONNOR**	NZ402747	RNZAF	*V-1*	**JN801**	SA-L	1.0	C
	F/L James H. **McCAW**	NZ414311	RNZAF	*V-1*	**EJ523**	SA-X	1.0	C
28.07.44	P/O Frank B. **LAWLESS**	NZ411417	RNZAF	*V-1*	**JN770**	SA-V	2.0	C
30.07.44	F/L James H. **McCAW**	NZ414311	RNZAF	*V-1*	**EJ523**	SA-X	1.0	C
03.08.44	W/O Owen D. **EAGLESON**	NZ421689	RNZAF	*V-1*	**JN808**	SA-N	2.0	C
	F/O Stamford S. **WILLIAMS**	NZ412297	RNZAF	*V-1*	**JN858**	SA-Y	2.0	C
	F/O William A. **HART**	NZ424461	RNZAF	*V-1*	**JN732**	SA-I	1.0	C
	P/O Robert D. **BREMMER**	NZ424417	RNZAF	*V-1*	**JN767**	SA-B	1.0	C
	F/O Neville J. **POWELL**	NZ415013	RNZAF	*V-1*	**JN808**	SA-N	1.0	C
04.08.44	W/O Owen D. **EAGLESON**	NZ421689	RNZAF	*V-1*	**EJ528**	SA-P	1.0	C
	W/O Brian J. **O'CONNOR**	NZ402747	RNZAF	*V-1*	**JN801**	SA-L	1.0	C
	P/O Keith A. **SMITH**	NZ403828	RNZAF	*V-1*	**JN821**	SA-H	3.0	C
05.08.44	F/O Henry M. **MASON**	NZ413104	RNZAF	*V-1*	**JN801**	SA-L	1.0	C
06.08.44	F/O James G. **WILSON**	NZ403555	RNZAF	*V-1*	**JN802**	SA-C	1.0	C
	W/O William A. **KALKA**	NZ415415	RNZAF	*V-1*	**EJ524**	SA-M	1.0	C
	P/O William A.L. **TROTT**	NZ417131	RNZAF	*V-1*	**EJ528**	SA-P	1.0	C
	F/O Raymond J. **DANZEY***	NZ416464	RNZAF	*V-1*	**JN803**	SA-D	0.5	C
	P/O Robert D. **BREMMER***	NZ424417	RNZAF	*V-1*	**EJ524**	SA-M	0.5	C
	F/O Raymond J. **CAMMOCK**	NZ414723	RNZAF	*V-1*	**EJ523**	SA-Z	1.0	C
	N.B: 150 Wing ORB gives 6 V-1s destroyed for 486 that day.							
07.08.44	F/O Raymond J. **CAMMOCK**	NZ414723	RNZAF	*V-1*	**JN863**	SA-R	1.0	C
09.08.44	F/L Harvey N. **SWEETMAN**	NZ40992	RNZAF	*V-1*	**EJ577**	SA-F	1.0	C
	F/L Lloyd J. **APPLETON**	NZ415213	RNZAF	*V-1*	**JN808**	SA-N	1.0	C

Some more of the squadron's pilots from the Tempest era:
Above left, F/L H.N. Sweetman completed a tour with 486 Sqn between March 1942 and July 1943, having previously served with 234 and 485 Squadrons from March 1941. He started a second tour with 486 in February 1944, leaving in September to command 3 Sqn (also flying Tempests). Above right, P/O B.M. Hall didn't get the chance to complete his first tour, begun in January 1944, as he was killed in action on 27.12.44.
Below left, F/L J.H. McCaw arrived at 486 in August during the early days of the Typhoon. He remained for the next two years and ended the war as a test pilot with D Napier & Sons, testing experimental engines. He survived the war. Below right, F/O B.J. O'Connor served with the squadron between December 1943 and May 1945.

Date	Pilot	Serial No.	Air Force	Enemy	Aircraft	Code	Score	
15.08.44	W/O Owen D. **Eagleson**	NZ421689	RNZAF	*V-1*	**EJ635**	SA-T	0.5	C
	Shared with a Tempest of 3 Sqn							
	F/O Raymond J. **Cammock**	NZ414723	RNZAF	*V-1*	**EJ528**	SA-P	1.0	C
	F/L Keith G. **Taylor-Cannon**	NZ412284	RNZAF	*V-1*	**JN808**	SA-N	1.0	C
16.08.44	F/Sgt John **Steedman**	NZ422328	RNZAF	*V-1*	**EJ528**	SA-P	2.0	C
	F/L Harvey N. **Sweetman**	NZ40992	RNZAF	*V-1*	**JN732**	SA-I	1.0	C
	W/O Owen D. **Eagleson**	NZ421689	RNZAF	*V-1*	**EJ635**	SA-T	3.0	C
	P/O Keith A. **Smith**	NZ403828	RNZAF	*V-1*	**JN808**	SA-N	1.0	C
	F/O William L. **Miller**	NZ402208	RNZAF	*V-1*	**JN803**	SA-D	1.0	C
18.08.44	F/O Neville J. **Powell**	NZ415013	RNZAF	*V-1*	**EJ523**	SA-Z	1.0	C
19.08.44	F/Sgt William J. **Campbell**	NZ422366	RNZAF	*V-1*	**JN802**	SA-C	1.0	C
23.08.44	W/O Cornelius J. **Sheddan**	NZ412358	RNZAF	*V-1*	**EJ577**	SA-F	1.0	C
27.08.44	F/L James R. **Cullen**	NZ416462	RNZAF	*V-1*	**JN770**	SA-V	1.0	C
28.08.44	P/O William A.L. **Trott**	NZ417131	RNZAF	*V-1*	**JN863**	SA-R	1.0	C
29.08.44	W/O Brian J. **O'Connor**	NZ402747	RNZAF	*V-1*	**EJ577**	SA-F	1.0	C
	P/O Keith A. **Smith**	NZ403828	RNZAF	*V-1*	**JN770**	SA-V	1.0	C
	F/O Bevan M. **Hall**	NZ421705	RNZAF	*V-1*	**JN803**	SA-D	0.5	C
	Shared with a Tempest of 3 Sqn							
	F/O Raymond J. **Cammock**	NZ414723	RNZAF	*V-1*	**JN863**	SA-R	1.0	C
	P/O John H. **Stafford**	NZ421783	RNZAF	*V-1*	**JN803**	SA-D	1.0	C
31.08.44	W/O Brian J. **O'Connor**	NZ402747	RNZAF	*V-1*	**JN803**	SA-C	1.0	C
30.09.44	F/O Stamford S. **Williams**	NZ412297	RNZAF	Bf109	**EJ715**	SA-B	1.0	C
26.11.44	F/L Keith G. **Taylor-Cannon**	NZ412284	RNZAF	Ju188	**EJ606**	SA-U	0.5	C
	F/O Stamford S. **Williams**	NZ412297	RNZAF		**EJ577**	SA-F	0.5	C
	P/O John **Steedman**	NZ422328	RNZAF		**JN869**	SA-R	1.0	P
25.12.44	F/O John H. **Stafford**	NZ421783	RNZAF	Me262	**EJ787**	SA-J	0.5	C
	P/O Robert D. **Bremmer**	NZ424417	RNZAF		**EJ523**	SA-D	0.5	C
27.12.44	F/L Eric W. **Tanner**	NZ415037	RNZAF	Fw190	**EJ541**	SA-T	1.0	C
				Bf109			1.0	P
	F/L Keith G. **Taylor-Cannon**	NZ412284	RNZAF	Fw190	**EJ828**	SA-Z	1.0	C
	F/O Keith A. **Smith**	NZ403828	RNZAF	Fw190	**EJ711**	SA-Q	1.0	C
	P/O Sydney J. **Short**	NZ42465	RNZAF	Fw190	**JN808**	SA-N	1.0	C
01.01.45	S/L Arthur E. **Umbers**	NZ404003	RNZAF	Fw190	**EJ577**	SA-F	1.0	C
				Bf109			1.0	C
	F/O William A.L. **Trott**	NZ417131	RNZAF	Fw190	**EJ606**	SA-U	1.0	C
	P/O Garnet J. **Hooper**	NZ431213	RNZAF	Fw190	**EJ750**	SA-B	1.0	C
	P/O Cornelius J. **Sheddan**	NZ412358	RNZAF	Fw190	**EJ748**	SA-I	1.0	C
14.01.45	F/O Colin J. **McDonald**	NZ412706	RNZAF	Bf109	**EJ755**	SA-A	1.0	C
23.01.45	F/O Raymond J. **Danzey**	NZ416464	RNZAF	Fw190	**NV715**	SA-F	1.0	P
	S/L Arthur E. **Umbers**	NZ404003	RNZAF	Bf109	**NV715**	SA-F	1.0	C
	F/O John H. **Stafford**	NZ421783	RNZAF	Bf109	**EJ706**	SA-M	0.5	C
	W/O Anthony H. **Bailey**	NZ417146	RNZAF		**EJ750**	SA-B	0.5	C
02.02.45	F/O John H. **Stafford**	NZ421783	RNZAF	Do217	**EJ523**	SA-D	0.33	C
	F/O Robert D. **Bremmer**	NZ424417	RNZAF		**NV719**	SA-E	0.33	C
	P/O Cornelius J. **Sheddan**	NZ412358	RNZAF		**NV952**	SA-K	0.33	C
22.02.45	F/L John H. **Stafford**	NZ421783	RNZAF	Bf109	**NV971**	SA-L	1.0	C
	F/O Andrew R. **Evans**	NZ427480	RNZAF	Bf109	**EJ714**	SA-W	1.0	C
24.02.45	S/L Keith G. **Taylor-Cannon**	NZ412284	RNZAF	Bf109	**NV706**	SA-J	1.0	C
	F/L Neville J. **Powell**	NZ415013	RNZAF	Bf109	**NV763**	SA-N	1.0	C
06.04.45	F/O Cornelius J. **Sheddan**	NZ412358	RNZAF	Ju87	**EJ711**	SA-Q	2.0	C
10.04.45	F/L Warren E. **Schrader**	NZ411944	RNZAF	Fw190	**SN129**	SA-M	1.0	C
12.04.45	F/L John H. **Stafford**	NZ421783	RNZAF	Fw190	**SN129**	SA-M	1.0	C
14.04.45	F/O Cornelius J. **Sheddan**	NZ412358	RNZAF	Fw190	**SN129**	SA-M	1.0	C
	F/O Sydney J. **Short**	NZ42465	RNZAF	Fw190	**NV651**	SA-R	0.5	C
	W/O William J. **Shaw**	NZ424528	RNZAF		**NV753**	SA-J	0.5	C
15.04.45	F/L Warren E. **Schrader**	NZ411944	RNZAF	Fw190	**NV969**	SA-A	2.0	C
	F/L Arthur I. **Ross**	NZ424523	RNZAF	Fw190	**SN176**	SA-N	1.0	C
	F/O Brian J. **O'Connor**	NZ402747	RNZAF	Fw190	**SN129**	SA-M	1.0	C

	F/O Andrew R. **Evans**	NZ427480	RNZAF	Fw190	**NV988**	SA-Y	1.0	C
	W/O Reginald J. **Atkinson**	NZ428068	RNZAF	Fw190	**EJ739**	SA-W	1.0	C
	W/O Glen **Maddaford**	NZ4211710	RNZAF	Fw190	**EJ888**	SA-X	1.0	C
	F/Sgt Ross A. **Melles**	NZ422538	RNZAF	Fw190	**NV753**	SA-J	1.0	C
16.04.45	F/L Cornelius J. **Sheddan**	NZ412358	RNZAF	Fw190	**SN129**	SA-M	0.5	C
	P/O William J. **Shaw**	NZ424528	RNZAF		**NV753**	SA-J	0.5	C
	F/L Warren E. **Schrader**	NZ411944	RNZAF	Fw190	**NV969**	SA-A	1.0	C
	F/L John W. **Reid**	NZ2073	RNZAF	Fw190	**NV753**	SA-J	1.0	C
21.04.45	S/L Warren E. **Schrader**	NZ411944	RNZAF	Bf109	**NV969**	SA-A	1.0	C
	F/O Andrew R. **Evans**	NZ427480	RNZAF	Fw190	**SN136**	SA-V	1.0	C
25.04.45	F/O Keith A. **Smith**	NZ403828	RNZAF	Me262	**EJ711**	SA-Q	1.0	C
28.04.45	F/L John W. **Reid**	NZ2073	RNZAF	Ju52	**EJ697**	SA-H	0.5	C
	F/O Owen D. **Eagleson**	NZ421689	RNZAF		**SN136**	SA-V	0.5	C
29.04.45	S/L Warren E. **Schrader**	NZ411944	RNZAF	Fw190	**NV969**	SA-A	1.0	C
				Bf109	**NV969**	SA-A	2.5	C
	W/O Neil D. **Howard**	Aus. 409307	RAAF		**EJ659**	SA-I	0.5	C
	F/O Owen D. **Eagleson**	NZ421689	RNZAF	Fw190	**SN176**	SA-N	1.0	C
	F/O Colin S. **Kennedy**	Aus. 423245	RAAF	Fw190	**JN802**	SA-Y	1.0	C
	F/O Andrew R. **Evans**	NZ427480	RNZAF	Fw190	**SN136**	SA-V	1.0	P
	F/O Colin J. **McDonald**	NZ412706	RNZAF	Fw190	**SN176**	SA-N	1.0	C
	F/L John W. **Reid**	NZ2073	RNZAF	Fw190	**EJ659**	SA-J	1.0	C
	W/O James R. **Duncan**	NZ427022	RNZAF	Fw190	**JN802**	SA-Y	1.0	C
	F/O Andrew R. **Evans**	NZ427480	RNZAF	Bf109	**SN136**	SA-V	1.0	C
01.05.45	S/L Warren E. **Schrader**	NZ411944	RNZAF	Bf109	**SN136**	SA-V	1.0	C
02.05.45	F/O Owen D. **Eagleson**	NZ421689	RNZAF	Fw44	**SN176**	SA-N	1.0	C
	P/O William J. **Shaw**	NZ424528	RNZAF	Fi156	**NV753**	SA-J	0.5	C
	W/O Neil D. **Howard**	Aus. 409307	RAAF		**EJ739**	SA-W	0.5	C
	P/O William J. **Shaw**	NZ424528	RNZAF	Fw190	**NV753**	SA-J	0.5	C
	W/O Neil D. **Howard**	Aus. 409307	RAAF		**EJ739**	SA-W	0.5	C
	S/L Cornelius J. **Sheddan**	NZ412358	RNZAF	EA	**SN129**	SA-M	0.5	C
	F/O David J. **Thomson**	Aus. 436437	RAAF		**EJ659**	SA-J	0.5	C
03.05.45	F/L Colin J. **McDonald**	NZ412706	RNZAF	Ju88	**SN176**	SA-N	1.0	C
	W/O James R. **Duncan**	NZ427022	RNZAF	Ju88	**JN802**	SA-Y	1.0	C

Total: 62.0 + 242.33 V-1s

**Claim not mentioned in 486 ORB - possibly never confirmed.*

S/L C.J. Sheddan with his two flight commanders in May 1945. Left, F/L C.J. MacDonald and, right, F/L A.I. Ross.
(CT Collection)

Cornelius James Sheddan
NZ412358

'Jimmy' Sheddan joined the RNZAF in April 1941. He was trained in New Zealand and sailed to the UK in January 1942. He was initially at Hullavington, before completing his training at 57 OTU, and at the end of September joined.485 (NZ) Squadron as an NCO. However his stay was short for in January 1943 he was transferred to No.1 Delivery Flight. In May he returned to operations being posted to No. 486 (NZ) Squadron, equipped with Typhoons. He was shot down by flak once on 3 October but was picked up after spending 19 hours in the Channel. In spring, 1944, 486 Squadron converted to Tempests and was soon employed in the V-1 hunt. In one fortnight, during June and July, he would claim 7 destroyed, one being shared, but had to crash-land. He was hospitalised for a month returning to the unit in time to claim another V-1. He was held back through illness when the squadron moved to the Continent, but did join them later in November. He opened his score on 1 January 1945 shooting down a Fw190, followed by more successes in February and April. He was promoted a flight commander, and awarded a DFC during May. On 2 May he was given command of the squadron, the same day that he made his last claim, a four-engine flying boat, which was shared. His score of seven confirmed victories included three which were shared, in addition to his eight V-1s (one shared), He continued command of the squadron until it was disbanded in September 1945, and left the RNZAF in April 1946.

Hawker Tempest Mk. V SN129
No. 486 (NZ) Squadron
Squadron Leader CJ Sheddan
B.158/Lübeck (Germany), summer 1945

'Jimmy' Sheddan in his last mount, SN129/SA-M.

Left, EJ712/SA-T photographed at Volkel in early October 1944. The D-Day stripes were at the time applied under the fuselage only. *(CT Collection)*

Middle left, The opposite side of NV753/SA-J, see p15. *(CT Collection)*

Below, photo taken from F/l J.W. Reid's cockpit of a section about to scramble at Kastrup. In the nearest Tempest JN807/SA-U with F/L F.P. Kendall on board (British) and behind EJ888/SA-X with P/O J.R. Duncan. *(JR Reid via P. Sortehaug)*

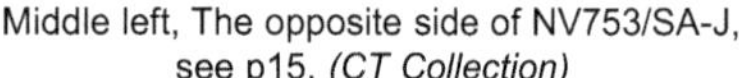

Some Tempests that participated to the V-1 campaign. Above EJ560/SA-M and, below, JN802/SA-Y. At the time, JN804 was coded 'SA-C'. JN802 left 486 Sqn in November 1944 and returned at the end of April 1945 to be coded 'SA-Y'. *(P. Sortehaug)*

Date	Pilot	S/N	Origin	Serial	Code	Fate
01.05.44	F/O James G. **WILSON**	NZ403555	RNZAF	**JN771**	SA-D	-
10.06.44	P/O Frank B. **LAWLESS**	NZ411417	RNZAF	**JN772**	SA-Q	-
22.06.44	F/O Thomas M. **FENTON**	NZ422273	RNZAF	**JN806**	SA-Q	-
28.06.44	P/O Frank B. **LAWLESS**	NZ411417	RNZAF	**JN859**	SA-S	-
	F/Sgt Roland J. **WRIGHT**	NZ421131	RNZAF	**JN804**	SA-R	†
30.06.44	F/Sgt Sydney J. **SHORT**	NZ42465	RNZAF	**JN810**	SA-P	-
01.07.44	P/O Kevin **MCCARTHY**	NZ417075	RNZAF	**JN773**	SA-C	Inj.
03.07.44	F/O William L. **MILLER**	NZ402208	RNZAF	**JN811**	SA-Z	-
04.07.44	F/O Stamford S. **WILLIAMS**	NZ412297	RNZAF	**JN820**	SA-P	-
05.07.44	W/O Cornelius J. **SHEDDAN**	NZ412358	RNZAF	**JN854**	SA-G	Inj.
20.07.44	F/Sgt Sydney J. **SHORT**	NZ42465	RNZAF	**EJ527**	SA-Q	-
23.07.44	P/O William A.L. **TROTT**	NZ417131	RNZAF	**JN758**	SA-Y	-
24.07.44	W/O William A. **KALKA**	NZ415415	RNZAF	**JN809**	SA-M	-
	F/O Neville J. **POWELL**	NZ415013	RNZAF	**JN860**	SA-J	-
31.07.44	P/O Alexander A. **WILSON**	NZ422336	RNZAF	**EJ586**	SA-Z	†
10.08.44	F/O Raymond J. **CAMMOCK**	NZ414723	RNZAF	**JN866**	SA-U	-
17.08.44	F/Sgt James W. **WADDELL**	NZ422335	RNZAF	**JN805**	SA-E	†
25.08.44	F/L Eric W. **TANNER**	NZ415037	RNZAF	**EJ625**	SA-T	-
06.10.44	F/O Raymond J. **CAMMOCK**	NZ414723	RNZAF	**JN863**	SA-R	†
07.10.44	F/O William A. **HART**	NZ424461	RNZAF	**EJ535**	SA-E	PoW
	W/O Anthony H. **BAILEY**	NZ417146	RNZAF	**EJ704**	SA-M	-
22.12.44	F/L Stamford S. **WILLIAMS**	NZ412297	RNZAF	**EJ715**	SA-B	†
26.12.44	F/O Colin J. **MCDONALD**	NZ412706	RNZAF	**EJ716**	SA-A	-
	P/O Brian J. **O'CONNOR**	NZ402747	RNZAF	**JN869**	SA-R	-
27.12.44	F/O Bevan M. **HALL**	NZ421705	RNZAF	**EJ627**	SA-E	†
13.01.45	S/L Arthur E. **UMBERS**	NZ404003	RNZAF	**EJ577**	SA-F	-
	P/O William A. **KALKA**	NZ415415	RNZAF	**EJ606**	SA-U	-
	F/L Lloyd J. **APPLETON**	NZ415213	RNZAF	**EJ752**	SA-H	Inj.
02.02.45	P/O Garnet J.M. **HOOPER**	NZ413231	RNZAF	**EJ787**	SA-L	PoW
08.02.45	F/L William L. **MILLER**	NZ402208	RNZAF	**EJ750**	SA-B	PoW
14.02.45	S/L Arthur E. **UMBERS**	NZ404003	RNZAF	**NV715**	SA-F	†
25.02.45	W/O Ronald C. **MACPHERSON**	NZ417222	RNZAF	**EJ523**	SA-D	PoW
25.03.45	F/O William A. **KALKA**	NZ415415	RNZAF	**NV981**	SA-A	†
26.03.45	P/O Anthony H. **BAILEY**	NZ417146	RNZAF	**NV932**	SA-U	†
13.04.45	S/L Keith G. **TAYLOR-CANNON**	NZ412284	RNZAF	**SN184**	SA-F	†
	F/Sgt Warren J.K. **HART**	NZ4211710	RNZAF	**EJ864**	SA-D	Inj.
14.04.45	W/O Owen J. **MITCHELL**	NZ424498	RNZAF	**SN141**	SA-U	†
15.04.45	F/O Andrew R. **EVANS**	NZ427480	RNZAF	**NV988**	SA-Y	-
24.04.45	F/Sgt Walter W. **MAY**	NZ44799	RNZAF	**NV651**	SA-R	PoW
26.04.45	F/O Keith A. **SMITH**	NZ403828	RNZAF	**NV967**	SA-Z	PoW
27.04.45	F/Sgt Ross A. **MELLES**	NZ422538	RNZAF	**EJ584**	SA-D	PoW
02.05.45	F/O Owen D. **EAGLESON**	NZ421689	RNZAF	**NV722**	SA-Q	Eva.
03.05.45	P/O John E. **WOOD**	NZ422339	RNZAF	**NV791**	SA-L	PoW
	P/O Charles E. **BLEE**	NZ438131	RNZAF	**EJ550**		Inj.
04.05.45	F/O Thomas McK. **AUSTIN**	NZ416896	RNZAF	**JN877**	SA-Y	PoW

Total: 45

Tempest EJ627/SA-E taking off during autumn 1944. This aircraft was shot down by Fw190s on 27 December 1944. Flying Officer B.M. Hall was killed.
A fitter working on EJ752/SA-H paused to warm his hands over a brazier at B.80/Volkel. Conditions for groundcrew were harsh during the winter of 1944/45 when most maintenance had to be carried out in the open. *(CT Collection)*

Returning from a sortie over Germany in the spring of 1945. Left to right, F/L JH Stafford, S/L KG Taylor-Cannon (†13.04.45), F/O OD Eagleson and F/L AR Evans.
(KA Smith via P. Sortehaug)

Summary of the aircraft lost by accident - 486 Squadron

Date	Pilot	S/N	Origin	Serial	Code	Fate
27.04.44	F/O Henry M. **Mason**	NZ413104	RNZAF	**JN792**		-
19.06.45	F/O Owen D. **Eagleson**	NZ421689	RNZAF	**NV969**	SA-A	-
27.08.45	P/O William J. **Shaw**	NZ424528	RNZAF	**EJ659**	SA-I	**Inj.**

Total: 3

'Rosie' Mackie joined the RNZAF in January 1941 and, upon completion of his training, arrived in the UK during the summer of 1941. Following OTU, he was posted to 485 (NZ) Squadron in August 1941. He made his first claim on 26 March 1942, sharing a Bf109 destroyed. He volunteered to serve in North Africa and, in January 1943, joined 243 Sqn in March, becoming a flight commander in April. The Tunisian campaign was raging at the time and, after a promising debut in UK, Mackie's score exploded during the spring of 1943. In May, he was awarded the DFC and in June he was promoted to command the squadron. More successes followed over Sicily and Italy and he added a Bar to his DFC in September. In November, he was posted out to command 92 Sqn until the end of February 1944 when he left Italy to return to the UK for a rest.

He returned to operations in December 1944, joining 274 Sqn as supernumerary squadron leader, flying Tempests. In January, he left 274 to command 80 Sqn, leading the unit until April when he was promoted to wing leader of 122 Wing, the only 2TAF wing formed with Tempest-equipped squadrons, where he would make his final claims, the very last in the air on 15 April. He continued to lead the wing until September by which time he had been made a Companion of the DSO (in May).

His final score was 23 confirmed victories (three shared), two probables and eleven damaged.

Hawker Tempest Mk V SN228
No. 122 Wing
Wing Commander ED Mackie
B.152/Fassberg (Germany), April-May 1945

Hawker Tempest Mk V SN228
No. 122 Wing
Wing Commander ED Mackie
B.152/Fassberg (Germany), summer 1945

When Mackie became the Wing Commander of 122 Wing, he acquired a new Tempest, SN228 which was coded 'EDM' and his scoreboard made at the time of 24 swatiskas and a single Italian marking.
At some time in the summer of 1945, a 122 Wing badge was added to the fin of SN228, bearing the original title of the unit '122 Airfield Headquarters'. The spinner was repainted, most probably in yellow.
(CT Collection)

Hawker Tempest Mk. V JN766
No. 486 (NZ) Squadron
Newchurch (UK), May 1944

Hawker Tempest Mk. V JN754
No. 486 (NZ) Squadron
Newchurch (UK), June 1944

Hawker Tempest Mk. V EJ712
No. 486 (NZ) Squadron
B.80/Volkel (Netherlands), October 1944

Hawker Tempest Mk. V NV753
No. 486 (NZ) Squadron
B.80/Volkel (Netherlands), March 1945

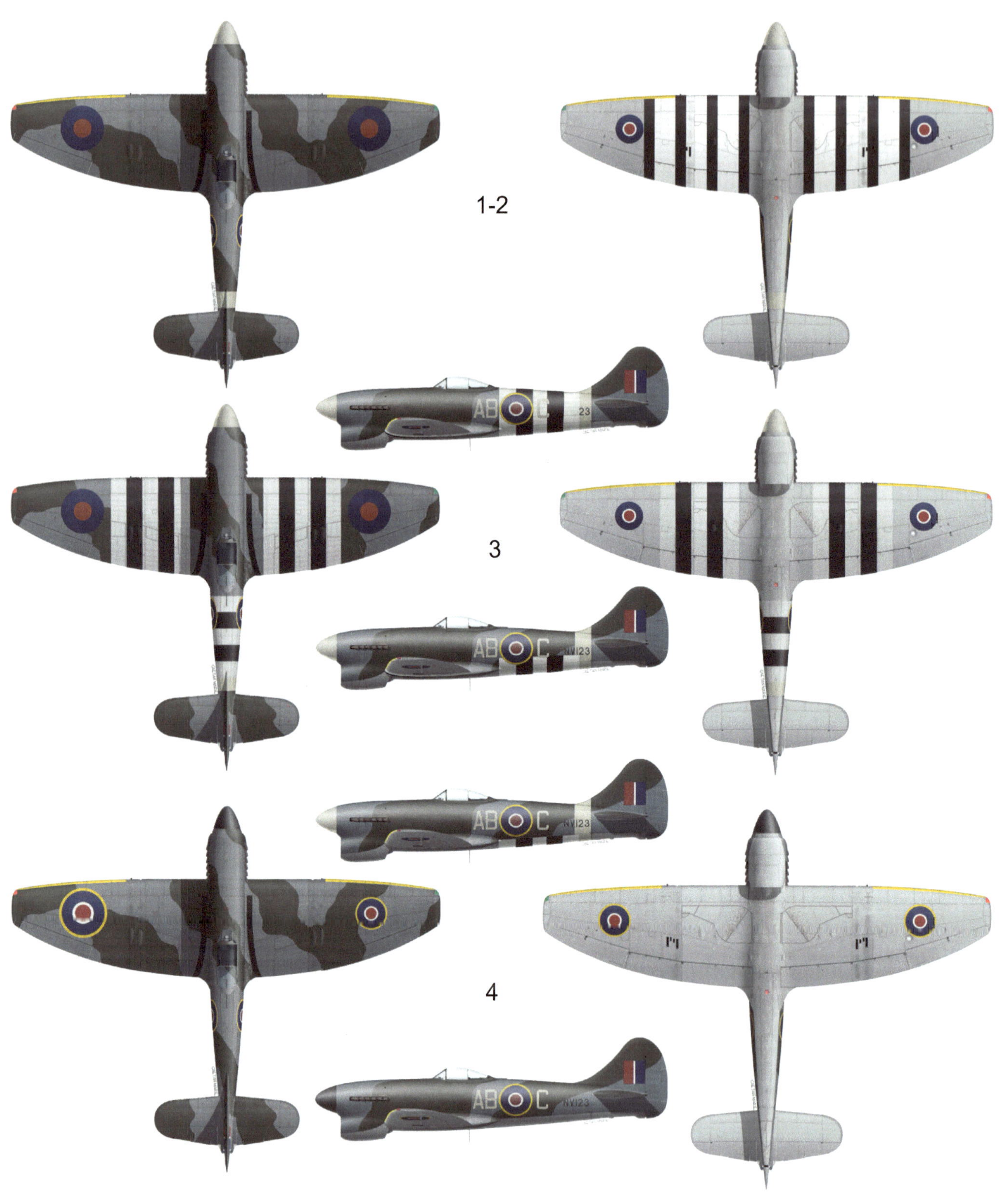

1-2. Basic scheme: Standard Day Fighter Scheme of a Dark Green and Ocean Grey with Medium Sea Gey undersides.Spinners painted in Sky. 18-inch wide Sky band on rear fuselage. Yellow wing leading edge stripes. Early Recognition stripes. Initially the Tempest was painted with alternating 12-inches Night and 24-inches White stripes on the wing undersurfaces. These were initially used on the Typhoon to facilitate the recognition of the new aircraft type, but by the time the Tempest entered service, orders had been given for the stripes to be removed on the Typhoon. Some sources indicate the stripes were 12 inches and 18 inches wide, but the proper size is 12 and 24. The outer stripes were aligned with the inboard border of the aileron.

3. Invasion stripes. Introduced around the 5th of June 1944, the invasion stripes consisted of 5 alternating white and black stripes of 18 inches in width on the wings and fuselage. Placement and application varied considerably. Later on invasion stripes stage 2 from July 6th ,1944, the invasion stripes were ordered removed from all upper surfaces. Invasion stripes stage 3, between 25 August and 10 September 1944, the underwing stripes were ordered removed.

4. 2nd Tactical Air Force. On 3 January 1945, the 2nd Tactical Air Force adopted new markings. Spinners were to be painted Night (reportedly this was the case since the creation of the 2nd Tactical Air Force, but most aircraft retained Sky spinners). All roundels were to be converted to National Marking II / C-type with the addition of a yellow ring. Underwing roundels were converted to 36-inch C1 types by the addition of a 2-inch yellow ring to the existing roundel. Upperwing roundels were either converted to 55-inch C1 types (version 6A) or overpainted, with 36-inch C1 types applied in their place (version 6B). Fuselage sky band was to be removed.

SQUADRONS! - The series

Donald James Matthew BLAKESLEE DFC
Supermarine Spitfire Mk.VB EN951
No. 133 (Eagle) Squadron
Flight Lieutenant D. J. M. Blakeslee
GAN. / J.4331
Gravesend (UK), August 1942

Charles Cuthbertson LEARMONTH DFC*
Douglas Boston Mk.III A28-6 (ex-AL891)
No. 22 Squadron RAAF
Squadron Leader C. C. Learmonth
Aus. 383
Port Moresby (New Guinea), spring 1943

Hans Anton MAURENBRECHER
Curtiss P-40N-35-CU C3-560
No. 120 (NEI) Squadron
Major H. Maurenbrecher
Biak (New Guinea), 1943-1944

Roland Prosper BEAMONT DSO* DFC*
Hawker Tempest Mk.V JN751
No. 150 Wing
Wing Commander R. P. Beamont
RAF No. 41809
Bradwell Bay (UK), April 1944

Ronald Thomas SUSANS DSO DFC
North American P-51D-25-NT A68-794
No. 77 squadron, RAAF
Squadron Leader R. T. Susans
O4391
Bofu (Japan), 1947

James Henry LACEY DFM*
Supermarine Spitfire Mk.XIV RN135
No. 17 Squadron
Squadron Leader J. H. Lacey
RAF No. 112709
Seletar (Singapore), autumn 1945

Introducing's RAF In Combat and Bravo Bravo Aviation's collection of
highly-detailed and historically accurate, high-quality aviation prints.
For more information on available prints, please visit :

or

Prints in connection with the book:

PL-001: ED Mackie (1)
PL-037: CJ Sheddan
PL-053: JH Ircmonger
PL-220: ED Mackie (2)
PL-229: ED Mackie (3)
PL-230: AE Umbers
PL-231: KG Taylor-Cannon
PL-232: WE Schrader

Evan Dall MACKIE DSO DFC*
Tempest Mk.V Series II SN228
No 122 Wing
Wing Commander E. D. Mackie
NZ41520
B.152/Fassberg (Germany), April-May 1945